THE FOOD STANDARDS AGENCY

A Force for Change

PREFACE   by the Prime Minister

FOREWORD   by the UK Agriculture and Health Ministers

		Page Numbers
Chapter 1	INTRODUCTION AND SUMMARY	1
Chapter 2	THE AGENCY'S GUIDING PRINCIPLES	4
Chapter 3	WHAT THE AGENCY SHOULD DO	8
Chapter 4	THE AGENCY'S ROLE IN FOOD SAFETY	17
Chapter 5	THE AGENCY'S ROLE IN FOOD STANDARDS AND NUTRITION	32
Chapter 6	THE AGENCY'S STRUCTURE AND ITS ACCOUNTABILITY	35
Chapter 7	THE AGENCY IN SCOTLAND, WALES AND NORTHERN IRELAND	40
Chapter 8	FINANCING THE AGENCY	43
Chapter 9	THE WAY AHEAD	46
Annex 1	The James Report	48
Annex 2	Existing Arrangements	65
	— Appendix 1 — Primary Legislation Affecting Food	68
	— Appendix 2 — Advisory Committees	71
Glossary		74

PREFACE BY THE PRIME MINISTER

This government took office committed to setting up an independent Food Standards Agency, which would be powerful, open and dedicated to the interests of consumers. Professor Philip James' report, which I received on 8 May, provided an excellent foundation on which to build this long-overdue reform.

Since then the Government has consulted widely, finding widespread support for change. This White Paper sets out proposals that will transform the way food standards issues are handled in this country. For too long, consumers in the United Kingdom have suffered from uncertainty and confusion about the quality and safety of the food they buy. Our food and farming industries have been damaged as a result.

The Government is determined to do away with the old climate of secrecy and suspicion and replace it with modern, open arrangements which will deliver real improvements in standards. This fresh approach will help to command the confidence of consumers, industry and our partners in the EU and beyond.

Tony Blair

TONY BLAIR

.1141685

THE FOOD STANDARDS AGENCY

A FORCE FOR CHANGE

C

Presented to Parliament by the

Minister of Agriculture, Fisheries and Food

by Command of Her Majesty

January 1998

Cм 3830   £10.50

FOREWORD BY THE UK AGRICULTURE AND HEALTH MINISTERS

Food safety is an issue which concerns every man, woman and child in this country. It is one of the Government's key priorities.

This White Paper sets out detailed proposals for a Food Standards Agency which will promote high standards throughout the food chain, from the point of production to the point of consumption. It will be a powerful new body, dealing with a complex area and a wide range of interest groups, from producers, manufacturers and retailers to scientific experts, public health professionals and, most importantly, consumers. The Agency will not be tied to any vested interests. It will have clearly defined priorities. It will be free to publish any of the advice it provides to Government. If Ministers decide not to follow that advice they will have to explain their reasons to the public and to Parliament.

The Government's proposals are detailed and comprehensive, but they do not answer all the questions which this radical new approach to food safety raises. We look forward to hearing views from all the stakeholders and discussing the implications of what is proposed over the next few weeks. The responses we receive will influence the drafting of the Bill to establish the Agency, which will itself be the subject of a further consultation exercise during 1998.

These proposals are fundamental to every citizen in the country. We are determined that our commitment to public consultation will ensure we get it right.

Jack Cunningham

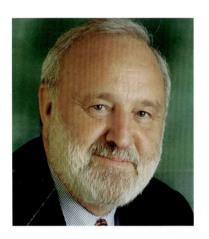

Frank Dobson

Donald Dewar

Ron Davies

Mo Mowlam

Chapter 1 :
Introduction and Summary

1.1 The Government is committed to introducing major changes in the arrangements for handling food safety and standards in the UK. It is determined to strengthen and open up the ways in which these issues are handled and thereby to improve food safety and to restore public confidence in the nation's food. This White Paper sets out the Government's detailed proposals for a powerful new body which will be responsible for protecting public health by promoting a safer food supply, and ensuring that consumers have the information they need to be able to choose a safe and healthy diet.

Summary of the proposals

1.2 These proposals are intended to deliver fundamental and lasting change in the way food safety and standards issues are handled by Government. They envisage an Agency with a clear focus on protecting the public and a powerful statutory remit across the whole food chain:

- at arm's length from Government and independent of sectoral interests
- governed by a Chairperson and Commission appointed openly on the basis of their personal standing and expertise
- operating under guiding principles which put the interest of the public unequivocally as the first priority
- able to make public its views on any issues related to food and public health
- taking a strategic view of food safety and standards issues across the whole food chain
- with wide-ranging powers to commission research and surveillance, propose legislation, monitor food law enforcement and take action to remedy problems
- with a clear responsibility to provide the public with information and advice.

1.3 The Agency will have protection of the public as its essential aim. It will be open and transparent in the way it works and will consult fully with all the interest groups affected by its activities. Its guiding principles will be laid down by law. They are designed to ensure that the Agency exercises its very considerable powers sensibly and responsibly, without compromising its duty to make protection of public health its first priority.

1.4 The Agency will be responsible for formulating policy and advising Government on the need for legislation on all aspects of food safety and standards and on certain aspects of nutrition. It will provide information and educational material for the public on food matters. It will work closely with Government Departments and other bodies with related responsibilities for protecting the public, in particular in areas such as nutrition and farming practices.

1.5 The Agency will obtain advice from the independent scientific Advisory Committees and will itself commission research and surveillance. It will base its decisions and actions on the best and most up to date scientific knowledge. It will work closely with the food industry to ensure that it keeps abreast of technological developments and to establish the best methods of delivering the high standards of safety and quality which consumers deserve.

1.6 The Agency will monitor the whole of the food chain, from the farm to the shop or restaurant. It will not take over the existing enforcement responsibilities of local authorities, but it will set standards for enforcement and will have powers to take action directly to protect the public, or to direct other bodies to do so, if there is a failure in the system.

1.7 The Agency will be accountable to Parliament through Health Ministers. It will be run by a Chairperson and Commission appointed on the basis of their personal standing and expertise. Commissioners will not be representatives of any particular sector or interest group. The Commission will be able to publish any of the advice that it gives to Government.

1.8   The Agency will advise the Government on the policy framework for standards and safety matters for the whole of the United Kingdom. Its headquarters will be in London, and there will be Food Standards Agency Executives in Scotland, Wales and Northern Ireland which will take over the existing food standards functions of the Scottish, Welsh and Northern Ireland offices. New Advisory Committees will be created in Scotland, Wales and Northern Ireland to advise Ministers in those countries, and the UK Agency, on the implications for Scotland, Wales and Northern Ireland of the Agency's proposals and actions and on any specific Scottish, Welsh or Northern Irish food safety and standards issues.

1.9   The Agency will be financed in part through transfer of the budgets for the functions which will become the Agency's responsibility and in part through charges on the food industry. The Government is considering possible mechanisms for transferring a higher proportion of the costs of food safety and standards work from the taxpayer to the food industry.

Why the Agency is needed

1.10   The Government believes that creation of the Food Standards Agency will put an end to the climate of confusion and suspicion which has resulted from the way food safety and standards issues have been handled in the past. This radical new approach will ensure that all future Government activity relating to food will be subject to public scrutiny, and that the public's voice will be fully heard in the decision making process.

1.11   The Government's proposals have been drawn up in the light of Professor Philip James's report and the responses to the consultation exercise carried out in May and June 1997 (described in Annex 1 of this White Paper). They are designed to address the key factors which Professor James identified as contributing to the erosion of public and producer confidence in the current system of food controls:

- the potential for conflicts of interest within MAFF arising from its dual responsibility for protecting public health and for sponsoring the agriculture and food industries
- fragmentation and lack of co-ordination between the various government bodies involved in food safety
- uneven enforcement of food law.

1.12   The Government agrees that a clear separation is needed between promoting safe food and wider consumer interests on the one hand and promoting the interests of business on the other.

1.13   Consultation shows that people find the present division of responsibilities between different departments of Government to be confusing. The Government agrees that greater clarity is needed. It believes that a better co-ordinated and more rational approach to food safety policy is essential. By giving central responsibility to a single body, whose essential aim is the protection of public health and which has the right to make its advice to Ministers public, the Government will ensure that the effectiveness of controls on food is not undermined by overlaps, conflicting objectives or incoherence. Where institutional barriers are found in the food chain, responsibilities will be clearly defined and better communication will be encouraged, both by building on the well-established networks that already exist — in particular at local level — and by fostering new links between those working in related fields.

1.14   Food law enforcement has been the subject of controversy in recent years. Concerns about over-zealous enforcement have distracted attention from the fundamental task of the enforcement authorities — to ensure that food businesses are complying with their obligations under the Food Safety Act. There is a real need for clearly focused, coherent guidance and support for enforcement officers on the ground, so that consumers and businesses throughout the United Kingdom can benefit from a consistent and proportionate inspection system.

1.15 Organisational change alone will not be sufficient to restore public confidence. Cultural change must also be achieved by demonstrating that protection of the public is the top priority, and by conducting business more openly and transparently, with greater public involvement in policy making and better clearer information reaching consumers.

1.16 These organisational and cultural changes can best be delivered by creating a new and powerful body, at arms length from Government and independent of the food industry, whose essential task is to protect the interests of the public, which operates in accordance with clearly defined and well understood guiding principles, and which is free to make public its advice to Ministers.

1.17 The Government is determined to ensure that the Agency has a firm and reliable foundation and that it can operate effectively in practice. This White Paper therefore invites detailed comments on the proposed arrangements.

1.18 Comments should be sent to the following address:

Mrs S Lamont
MAFF/DH Joint Food Safety and
Standards Group
Ergon House
c/o Nobel House
17 Smith Square
London SW1P 3JR

1.19 Respondents in Scotland, Wales and Northern Ireland should reply to the Scottish, Welsh or Northern Irish contact, as follows:

Mr J Bannatyne
The Scottish Office Food Group
Pentland House
47 Robb's Loan
Edinburgh
EH14 1TY

Mr I Jackson
Welsh Office Public Health Division
Cathays Park
Cardiff
CF1 3NQ

Mr T Robinson
Health and Social Policy Unit
Department of Health and Social Services
Annex 4
Castle Buildings
Stormont
Belfast BT4 3SP

1.20 The Government may wish to publish these comments or make them available to others. Respondents who wish their comments to be treated in confidence should make this clear in any papers they submit.

1.21 The closing date for responses to this White Paper is 16 March 1998.

Chapter 2:
The Agency's Guiding Principles

2.1 The Government's aim in setting up the Agency is to strengthen food safety and standards policies and procedures so as to rebuild the public's trust in the machinery for handling food issues. This aim will only be achieved if the Agency's policies and procedures are consistent and transparent and it is clear to the public that, where costs and benefits have to be weighed, the Agency will do this in the context that its essential aim is to protect public health. This Chapter describes the context in which the Agency will operate and sets out the principles which the Government proposes should guide its activities.

2.2 The Agency is being established at a time when food safety policies are coming under increasing scrutiny nationally and internationally. The use of science in policy making more generally is developing fast at a global level. The Agency will need to draw up and communicate an overall approach to risk analysis and decision making which will enable it to maintain a coherent and consistent policy while participating in and responding to these wider developments.

2.3 The guiding principles within which the Agency will operate will be an important element in securing public confidence. These principles will be set out in the legislation establishing the Agency and in its Management Statement. The legislation will provide Ministers with powers to issue directions to the Agency to prevent it from acting in a manner which contravenes its guiding principles. These powers of direction will not be able to be used to prevent the Agency from making and publishing recommendations which may simply be unpopular with the Government. Rather the intention is to provide a measure of democratic accountability should the Agency seek to act in a manner which is inconsistent with its legislative framework.

2.4 The proposed guiding principles for the Agency are set out below. They are designed to recognise the need, in the food safety area as in other areas of public policy, to assess, manage and communicate risk effectively and in a transparent manner. The Government would welcome comments on these proposed principles.

The Guiding Principles

(1) The essential aim of the Agency is the protection of public health in relation to food.

(2) The Agency's assessments of food standards and safety will be unbiased and based on the best available scientific advice, provided by experts invited in their own right to give independent advice.

(3) The Agency will make decisions and take action on the basis that:
— the Agency's decisions and actions should be proportionate to the risk; pay due regard to costs as well as benefits to those affected by them; and avoid over-regulation;
— the Agency should act independently of specific sectoral interests.

(4) The Agency will strive to ensure that the general public have adequate, clearly presented information in order to allow them to make informed choices. In doing this, the Agency will aim to avoid raising unjustified alarm.

(5) The Agency's decision making processes will be open, transparent and consultative, in order that interested parties, including representatives of the public:
— have an opportunity to make their views known;
— can see the basis on which decisions have been taken;
— are able to reach an informed judgement about the quality of the Agency's processes and decisions.

(6) Before taking action, the Agency will consult widely, including representatives of those who would be affected, unless the need for urgent action to protect public health makes this impossible.

(7) In its decisions and actions, the Agency will aim to achieve clarity and consistency of approach.

(8) The Agency's decisions and actions will take full account of the obligations of the UK under domestic and international law.

(9) The Agency will aim for efficiency and economy in delivering an effective operation.

2.5 These guiding principles would have a number of important implications for the Agency's methods of operation.

2.6 Food safety policies are designed to ensure that food production, processing and distribution systems deliver food which is safe and wholesome. However, complete freedom from risk is an unattainable goal, and safety and wholesomeness are related to the level of risk that society regards as reasonable in the context of, and in comparison with, other risks in everyday life. In assessing and managing risks, the Agency will need to take very careful account of the expectations of the consumer, recognising that in many circumstances the public is unlikely to be willing to pay the cost of achieving the maximum theoretical level of safety (whether that cost is manifested in higher food prices or in restrictions on freedom of choice).

2.7 Risk assessment needs to be based on the best available methodology, drawing on expert scientific advice and making appropriate allowances for the inevitable uncertainties involved. The available scientific data may be incomplete and difficult to interpret, thus making it very difficult to establish with certainty the nature and degree of risk. Where there are uncertainties about the scientific evidence, an element of political judgement is inevitably involved in reaching decisions on the best course of action. Where there is a risk of serious damage to public health, lack of full scientific certainty should not be used as a reason for postponing cost effective measures to reduce the health risks. Where it is not possible to identify a safe threshold level of intake in relation to an identified hazard, any risk from exposure should be reduced to as low a level as is reasonably practicable.

2.8 The best available scientific advice will need to take full account of technological and scientific developments in the UK and internationally. In some cases, it will lie within industry or other organisations with an interest in the Agency's advice and decisions. Experts from such organisations would be required to make clear public declarations of interest, and might need to be excluded from involvement in some specific cases or decisions, for example when serving on an Advisory Committee.

2.9 In assessing costs and benefits the Agency will need to take account of the effects of its actions on those affected (industry, enforcement authorities and other interested parties as well as consumers) against the background of its essential aim of protecting public health. It will need to take account of the benefit to consumers as a whole of being able to make informed choices from a wide range of food. On occasion it will need to balance the costs and benefits to different groups of consumers. For example a product may carry a significant risk to a specific group such as people with an allergy, but little or no risk to the generality of consumers. In such cases the Agency would need to consider alternative solutions, such as the provision of advice and information.

2.10 Since it is the food industry which will have the main responsibility for delivering food which meets the safety and quality standards set by the Agency, it will be essential for the Agency to secure the confidence, support and co-operation of all sectors of the industry as well as of the public at large. The Agency will need to be able to call on the industry's own scientific and process expertise, and to be trusted with confidential information about the industry's commercial developments, so that it has the maximum understanding of developments within its remit.

2.11 Responsible food producers, retailers and caterers already regard their customers' safety as an ethical and commercial priority, as is shown by the widespread welcome from many in the food industry for the proposal to transfer food safety responsibilities to an independent Agency to provide a clear focus on protection of the consumer. Subject always to the need for the Agency to be able to take emergency action, the interests of the consumer will be served best if the Agency and the food industry work closely together to establish methods of achieving the standards which the public interest requires.

2.12 Confidence in the new arrangements will only be achieved if the general public has access to information provided by the Agency on its own activities (including the basis for its decisions and actions and the decision-making process itself).

2.13 The Agency will comply with legislation and codes of practice on freedom of information. It will have regard for legitimate commercial and academic confidentiality but will publish information where there is a clear need for this to be in the public domain.

2.14 The Agency will be required to operate to the good practice required of Government Departments. Amongst other things, it will be required to undertake regulatory appraisal, including assessing the risks and ensuring that proposed legislation is proportionate. It will be required to follow the best practice principles set out in the Better Regulation Guide and the Regulatory Appraisal Guide. It is also intended that the Agency will follow the guidelines published by the Office of Science and Technology on the use of scientific advice in policy making.

Chapter 3:
What the Agency should do

3.1   This Chapter summarises the proposed scope of the Agency's responsibilities, and the functions which the Government proposes that it should discharge. The Government's detailed proposals on individual subject areas are set out in Chapters 4 and 5.

3.2   In summary, the proposal is that the Agency should take over responsibility from the Agriculture and Health Departments for advising Ministers on the UK policy framework in the areas of food safety and food standards, including important aspects of nutrition. This would include advising on the need for and content of legislation and the implementation of policy. The Agency should also have important responsibilities for public information and education on food matters, for representing the UK in the EU and other international organisations, for commissioning research and surveillance and for setting and monitoring standards for food law enforcement.

3.3   In some areas such as nutrition policy and food safety issues which relate to farming practices, Health, Agriculture and Environment Departments will retain important policy and statutory responsibilities. It will be necessary to define the relationship between the Agency and these Departments and to put in place mechanisms for co-ordination and collaboration which will allow the Agency effectively to discharge its responsibility to protect the public interest. Although it is important for the Agency to be at arms length from Government, it must not operate in isolation from those Departments and other bodies with responsibility for protection of the public.

3.4   The Government believes that if the Agency is to achieve the objective of strengthening and opening up the Government machinery for handling food-related issues it must be given a wide ranging remit, and it must have executive as well as advisory powers. An advisory body dealing only with food safety issues would not constitute an adequate response to the level of public concern which exists. Consumer interests in food encompass issues relating to the compositional quality of food, the choice of foods available and the information on which choices can be made. Compositional and labelling issues are also important factors in determining fair conditions of trade on the national and international market. The proposal to include food standards within the Agency's remit would therefore require it to work closely with the food industry to ensure that the public interest is properly protected in this important area.

3.5   The table opposite summarises the Agency's proposed responsibilities, including in the areas where Health, Agriculture and Environment Departments will retain some of their existing responsibilities. Further detail on all these areas is contained in the rest of this Chapter and in Chapters 4 and 5.

Table 1: The Agency's Functions

	Reference	Formulate policy	Draft secondary legislation	Negotiate in EU and internationally	Provide advice/ guidance/ information	Carry out research and surveillance	Set standards & monitor enforcement	Issue licences/ approvals/ authorisations
		Chapter 2 3.6-3.9	Chapter 2 3.6-3.9 (Note 1)	3.10-3.19	3.20-3.22	3.23-3.34	3.35-3.47	Chapter 4
Pathogens in live animals	4.9-4.13 (Note 2)	✓	✓	✓	✓	✓	✓	
Animal Feed	4.14-4.22 (Note 3)	✓		✓	✓	✓	✓	✓
Pesticides & Veterinary Medicines	4.23-4.32 (Note 4)				✓	✓		
Food Hygiene	4.33-4.36	✓	✓	✓	✓	✓	✓	
Meat & Milk Hygiene	4.37-4.43	✓	✓	✓	✓	✓	✓	✓
Food-borne Illness	4.44-4.52 (Note 5)	✓	✓	✓	✓	✓	✓	
Novel Foods & Processes	4.53-4.55	✓	✓	✓	✓	✓	✓	✓
Food Additives	4.56-4.57	✓	✓	✓	✓	✓	✓	✓
Chemical Contaminants	4.58-4.60 (Note 6)	✓	✓	✓	✓	✓	✓	
Radiological Safety	4.61-4.64 (Note 6)	✓	✓	✓	✓	✓	✓	
Food Intolerance	4.65-4.66	✓	✓	✓	✓	✓	✓	
Food Emergencies	4.67-4.68	✓	✓	✓	✓	✓	✓	
Food Standards (including labelling)	5.2-5.5	✓	✓	✓	✓	✓	✓	
Nutrition	5.6-5.15 (Note 7)	✓	✓	✓	✓	✓	✓	

(1) Using the enabling powers in the Food Safety Act 1990 and the Food Safety (Northern Ireland) Order 1991.

(2) Working closely with the Agriculture Departments to co-ordinate activity under the Food Safety Act 1990 and the Animal Health Act 1981.

(3) Working closely with Agriculture Departments who will retain the lead on aspects of animal feedingstuffs controls where food safety is not the primary concern.

(4) PSD/VMD will retain lead responsibility. The Agency will participate fully in the authorisation/licensing processes, will be consulted on policy, legislation and EU negotiations and will have powers to carry out its own surveillance for residues.

(5) Working closely with Health Departments on outbreak management and control policies and with PHLS eg on aspects of surveillance.

(6) The Agency will be a statutory consultee of the Environment Agency on applications for authorisation of discharges.

(7) Working closely with Health Departments, who will retain responsibility for wider public health issues including health surveillance of the population and will share responsibility with the Agency for defining the public health education message and for surveillance of the nutritional status of people.

Policy formulation and legislation

3.6 The consultation process has already highlighted a variety of issues where interest groups would like to see changes in the way policy is formulated and the existing legal controls are interpreted and applied, as well as some areas where these existing legal controls are considered to be inadequate.

3.7 In establishing the Agency the Government intends to remedy any gaps in the existing legal structure. Some areas which may require amendment are referred to in the following sections. The Government would welcome comments on any areas where the existing primary legislation is demonstrably deficient. It would be helpful if such comments included specific examples illustrating the deficiency which needs to be addressed.

3.8 The Government does not intend to prejudge the decisions which the Agency will need to take for itself about the way in which it implements and applies the legal controls which Parliament has put in place. The Agency will need to develop its own policies and procedures, within the constraints of the legislation and acting in accordance with its guiding principles (Chapter 2).

3.9 Secondary legislation will be made and presented to Parliament by Health Ministers or their successors under Devolution, acting on the advice of the Agency. The Agency will be responsible for preparing the statutory instrument, and for carrying out consultation with interested parties (including Government Departments). In considering the need for and content of new secondary legislation the Agency will be required to operate in accordance with its guiding principles and with the best practice guidelines which apply to Government Departments (see Chapter 2).

Involvement with the EU and other international bodies

3.10 The James Report envisaged that officials of the Agency would act as "technical advisers" in EU negotiations, rather than as representatives of the UK Government. The report observed that creation of the Agency at a time when the European Commission is reorganising its food standards, quality and safety activities provides an opportunity for the UK to play a major role in shaping future European food policy.

3.11 The Agency will be responsible for the provision of advice and for proposing and implementing legislation on the matters which fall within its remit (most of which are subject to EU competence). Staff of the Agency will therefore be the appropriate experts to represent the United Kingdom at working level in negotiations in the EU and other international fora. This reflects the current (and successful) practice for health and safety legislation, where officials from the Health and Safety Executive (HSE) represent the United Kingdom at working level in the EU and other fora. As the James Report recognised, ultimate policy responsibility for negotiations with the EU must rest with Ministers. The Agency will therefore need to ensure that negotiating lines are agreed with the appropriate Ministers, in accordance with the accountability arrangements described in Chapter 6. Where matters which are the responsibility of the Agency are normally dealt with in a meeting of the Council of Ministers in which a Departmental Minister other than the Secretary of State for Health takes the lead (for example the Minister of Agriculture, Fisheries and Food in the Agriculture Council or DTI Ministers in the Consumer Council and the Internal Market Council), the Agency will provide briefing to the relevant Minister.

3.12 EU negotiations and subsequent implementation of EC legislation in the UK can have policy implications which extend beyond the responsibilities of any individual Department or

Agency. Whitehall-wide communication and co-ordination mechanisms on EU matters already exist to ensure that all UK interests are taken into account in determining the UK policy line. Staff of the Agency will participate in these mechanisms. Where necessary — particularly if there is any disagreement between the Agency and Government Departments over the line to be taken in a particular EU negotiation — co-ordination of the UK line would take place through the normal Cabinet Office machinery including Ministerial and official Cabinet committees.

3.13 The European Commission has recently made changes to bring together non-legislative responsibilities on consumer protection and public health in relation to food into Directorate General XXIV under the responsibility of the Commissioner for consumer policy and health protection. DG XXIV also has responsibility for the relevant scientific committees in the food safety area, which play an increasingly important role in determining EU-wide food safety policy. The Agency will need to establish good working relations with DG XXIV and its committees as well as with other relevant parts of the Commission. It will also need to establish good communication mechanisms with members of the European Parliament.

Other international negotiations

3.14 The Agency will have responsibility in areas which are dealt with in other international fora such as the World Health Organisation (WHO), the Food and Agriculture Organisation (FAO), and the Codex Alimentarius. The same basic principles of co-ordination, consultation and representation will apply in these fora as in EU negotiations.

The Codex Alimentarius Commission

3.15 The Codex Alimentarius Commission, a body sponsored by the FAO and WHO, draws up international food safety standards which are recognised by the World Trade Organisation for the settlement of trade disputes. These standards are therefore very important for maintaining consumer protection in relation to imported products.

3.16 The Agency will represent the UK on the Codex Commission. It will seek advice or representation from MAFF, DH and other Government Departments in the work of the various specialist committees. The Government expects that the Agency will seek to increase the transparency of Codex work and encourage the participation of consumer representatives.

World Trade Organisation

3.17 The Agency's guiding principles will require it to respect the UK's international obligations, including adherence to the international trade rules of the World Trade Organisation (WTO). The WTO Agreements on Sanitary and Phytosanitary Measures (the SPS Agreement) and Technical Barriers to Trade (the TBT Agreement) provide for trade-related measures to protect human, animal and plant life and health but aims to prevent their use as a disguised barrier to international trade. As the Government's source of expertise on food safety matters, the Agency may be involved as appropriate in relevant SPS and TBT Agreement matters.

3.18 In the event of food-related trade disputes, relating to action by the UK, the EC or by third countries, the Agency will be a source of expert advice to the Government.

Organisational implications for the Agency

3.19 The Agency will need to establish a small team of staff to act as co-ordinators on EU and other international matters and to liaise as appropriate with Government Departments.

Public Information and Education

3.20 The James Report proposes a strong media and public information role for the Agency, including health education on food matters.

3.21 The Government agrees that the Agency should take a high profile role in providing information to the public, in accordance with the guiding principles set out in Chapter 2. The Agency will proceed on the basis of openness and transparency and will be within the scope of the Government's proposed Freedom of Information Act, details of which are set out in the White Paper "Your Right to Know: Freedom of Information" (Cm 3818).

3.22 The Agency will:

- establish its own communication strategy and have its own dedicated Communications Unit, including press and publicity experts and experts in risk communication. It will build on the work of the new MAFF/DH Risk Communication Unit, which it will subsume
- take over responsibility for and build on the food safety communications activities already developed in MAFF, DH and in Scotland, Wales and Northern Ireland, for example by the provision and development of advice, information and literature for the general public, such as the Food Safety Information Bulletin, the Consumer Help-line and the FoodSense series
- develop appropriate mechanisms for effective two-way exchange of information with the public at large, consumer organisations, industry, enforcement bodies and the media, for example by building on the work done by MAFF's Consumer Panel
- devise appropriate systems for improving its understanding of consumer opinion on food safety and standards matters to inform its own policy development and communications

- act as a source of expert advice to the Education Departments on food matters, including encouraging them to consider particular initiatives which might improve public understanding of food safety matters
- liaise with DH, HSE and other relevant bodies in promoting a coherent overall approach to health risk communication, building on experience gained in other policy areas. Staff of the Agency will participate in fora such as the Inter-Departmental Liaison Group on Risk Assessment (ILGRA) and the Inter-Departmental Group on Public Health (IDGPH)
- contract with the Health Education Authority and other health education bodies or agents, including the relevant body in Wales, to undertake health promotion and education activities relevant to nutrition, diet and food safety.

Research and Surveillance

3.23 The James Report recommended that the Agency should have responsibility for co-ordinating all research in the areas of food safety, nutrition and consumer protection. It proposed that the Agency's budget should include all the Government's spend on research and surveillance relating to these areas. The Report also recommended that a member of the Agency's Commission should sit on the Biotechnology and Biological Sciences Research Council (BBSRC) to provide a link with its research programme.

3.24 The consultation responses recognised the value of the Agency acting as a single reference point for research on food-related matters. However, a number of respondents were concerned about the proposal that the Agency should take on all basic research in addition to its needs for surveillance, monitoring and applied research. These respondents saw dangers in concentrating too much Research and Development (R & D), and its funding, in one place and advantages in funding of basic research in these areas remaining with the Research Councils (BBSRC and the Medical Research Council (MRC)). Respondents stressed that the Agency's research budget should reflect the scope of its responsibilities and that funding should not be reduced as a result of the creation of the Agency. The responses indicated a high level of interest in publicity for research findings, transparency, peer review of research results and accountability. Some argued that the Agency would require its own technical support, for example for chemical and microbial analysis. Others felt that there was no case for the Agency to own research facilities or conduct its R & D in-house.

3.25 The Government agrees that it is essential for the Agency to base its policies and decisions on the best possible science, achieved through openness, peer review and where possible by competition between research providers.

3.26 The Agency's scientific activities will encompass research commissioned to support policy, surveillance programmes, and the need to respond appropriately to emergencies from time to time. As part of its advice and public information responsibilities, the Agency will need to assess and communicate its long term needs for research, and contribute to strategic discussions about the food science base. It will need to keep abreast of scientific and technological developments relevant to its responsibilities in this country and internationally. It will need to make an appropriate scientific input into EU and international debate, for example, in WHO and Codex and to influence the research programmes in the food area being developed by the European Commission.

3.27 The Government strongly agrees that the Agency should be open and consultative in its approach to research. Research and surveillance play a key role in providing information on the safety, nutritional value and authenticity of food in order to inform and support regulation and enable

consumers to make informed choices. The Agency will need to commission research on the nature and magnitude of risks associated with its regulatory work including analysis of costs and benefits.

3.28 The Government agrees with the many comments which stressed the need to maintain the plurality of science funding. Basic and strategic research will continue to be funded by Research Councils and carried out by Research Council Institutes, other Institutes and Universities as at present.

3.29 Some areas of research and development which fall within MAFF's ongoing role of sponsorship of the food industry will continue to be funded by Agriculture Departments, especially programmes concerned with food technology and processing, and LINK programmes involving industry funding. The Agency will clearly need to work closely with MAFF and other research funders to ensure continuity throughout the food chain. Some research programmes currently funded by and through Agriculture and Health Departments are relevant to the responsibilities of both the Agency and the Departments. These borderline programmes will be reviewed, and decisions taken on a case by case basis whether they should become the responsibility of the Agency. The research and development programme of the Public Health Laboratory Service (PHLS) will need to be looked at in this context, though it would not be appropriate for research and development which directly supports the operational work of PHLS to be transferred to the Agency.

3.30 Close co-ordination between all funders of research in the food area will be essential if the Agency is to be able to draw on the full range of the best available scientific advice, whether or not funded directly by the Agency. This will require the fullest possible exchange of information, including details of research projects and results. This will enable the Agency to have access to the full range of relevant research work, prevent overlaps and gaps, and help to secure the best value for money. There are several possible models for co-ordination. The Government sees merit in establishing R & D Consultative Committees involving the main UK research sponsors covering broad areas such as microbiological safety of food, chemical safety of food, nutrition etc. The Government will consult further with appropriate interests to develop detailed proposals on the role, structure and composition of these committees, (including proposals for consumer representation).

3.31 The Agency may need to develop particularly close relations with the BBSRC. The President of the Board of Trade is responsible for appointments to the BBSRC Council and will consider its membership in the light of the personal experience and expertise which an appointment from the Agency could bring. Research Council appointments are not made to give representation to any particular body.

3.32 The precise amount of research funding to be transferred to the Agency will depend upon commitments to current research programmes, decisions on the borderline programmes referred to in paragraph 3.29, decisions on planned research and work coming to an end at the point the Agency is established. The relevant current research programmes of the Agriculture and Health Departments indicate that total annual research funding of about £25 million is likely to be transferred to the Agency.

3.33 The Agency will be committed to the research contracts which transfer to it. It will of course be for the Agency to determine its own priorities and procedures for future research once it is established. The Government anticipates that it will continue to commission research competitively, and to publish its own research strategy.

3.34 The Government agrees that the Agency should take over responsibility for most of the wide range of surveillance work undertaken by MAFF.

Surveys provide valuable information on the safety, authenticity and nutritional value of the UK food supply and form an essential element in the development of policies in these areas. An important component of the surveillance budget is spent on establishing dietary intakes of foods and nutrients by both the general population and also special groups within it. The total expenditure on surveys and related activities is over £6 million.

Food law enforcement

3.35 Professor James noted that the process of local authority food law enforcement had many strengths, and recommended that wherever possible the Agency should seek to ensure the effectiveness of local authority actions rather than take them over. He noted that there was a need to raise standards of food law enforcement and to ensure a consistent approach across the UK. He acknowledged that competition within individual authorities for funding of services contributes to the difficulty of maintaining consistency.

3.36 Professor James recommended as follows:

- The Agency should be responsible for co-ordinating, monitoring and auditing local authority enforcement activities
- It should have statutory powers to require local authorities to carry out certain work
- A local authority liaison unit should be established in the Agency to provide advice, guidance and support to enforcement officers
- The Agency should have reserve powers to take enforcement action, as well as direct enforcement responsibilities in the field of meat and milk hygiene
- The Agency could provide a resource to local authorities by taking over unusually complex litigation where it is unreasonable for an individual authority or groups of authorities to proceed
- The Agency should take over LACOTS' role as the Single Liaison Body for the United Kingdom within the EU

- The structures for assessing the chemical safety of food (the Public Analyst Service) in England and Wales should be reviewed as a matter of priority
- A unified Scottish Scientific Service should be established, covering both micro-biological and chemical food surveillance in Scotland.

3.37 During the consultation exercise there was widespread support for the recommendation that the Agency should oversee local authority enforcement activities rather than take them over. It was generally accepted that the Agency should set and monitor standards and audit local authorities' enforcement activities. Local authority respondents were concerned that the standards set by the Agency should not be over prescriptive but should allow for flexibility to take account of local circumstances. Many local authority respondents opposed the proposal that the Agency should have reserve statutory powers.

3.38 There was general support for the recommendation that the Agency should have a local authority liaison unit, and a variety of suggestions were made on how such a unit might be constituted and operated. There was no consensus on the future role of LACOTS; some respondents wished to see its role strengthened, while others proposed that its food safety and standards co-ordination work should be transferred to the Agency.

3.39 The recommendation for a review of Public Analyst services in England and Wales was generally welcomed. There was also wide support for the recommendation that food-related scientific services in Scotland should be reviewed and rationalised.

3.40 Many respondents recognised the difficulties over funding for local authority enforcement. Views differed on the desirability of ring-fencing of funding and its allocation through the Agency. (In Northern Ireland the additional funding made available to district councils following the introduction of the Food Safety (Northern Ireland) Order 1991 is already ring-fenced).

3.41 The Government agrees that general food law enforcement benefits from inspectors' local knowledge and that there are therefore good reasons why local authorities should retain their current enforcement responsibilities. However, it accepts Professor James's view that the effectiveness of enforcement could be reinforced by firmer co-ordination and oversight. It therefore agrees that the Agency needs to be in a position to exercise influence over individual authorities' enforcement activity and that it should have a proactive role in encouraging consistency across the United Kingdom.

3.42 The Government's proposals for the funding of local authority enforcement activity are discussed in Chapter 8 below. The proposals on meat and milk hygiene enforcement are described in Chapter 4 below.

3.43 The Government intends to enter into detailed discussion with local authority representative organisations and other interested parties on how the Agency and the local authorities can work together to improve consistency and, where necessary, to remedy any deficiencies in enforcement activity by individual authorities.

3.44 These discussions will build on the work which has been done by Health and Agriculture Departments, LACOTS, the Scottish Food Co-ordinating Committee and the Food Liaison Group of the Northern Ireland Chief Environmental Health Officers' Group in providing advice, guidance and support to local authorities, setting general standards for enforcement, and monitoring enforcement activity to encourage consistency. The BSE Regulatory Forum is one example of such work. Areas of activity which might be developed further include:

- formalising the Home Authority arrangements (under which the local authority for the main site of a multi-site business determines the acceptability of the company's food safety and standards controls and this determination is accepted by other authorities)

- making participation in these arrangements mandatory for all authorities
- specifying national standards of performance with appropriate indicators which are capable of being audited by the Agency, and publishing the results of such auditing
- better co-ordination of surveillance and monitoring programmes to meet both local and national needs
- developing the present regional liaison arrangements for trading standards work and encouraging local authorities to pool resources for the provision of technical and scientific specialist support
- overseeing the training and qualifications of food inspectors.

3.45 In order to ensure that the Agency is able to exercise real influence over individual local authorities' activities, and where necessary to take action to remedy deficiencies, it will be necessary to consider whether the powers in the Food Safety Act 1990 and the Food Safety (Northern Ireland) Order 1991 are adequate. For example, the Government is considering whether any of the following would be appropriate:

- new mechanisms to ensure that food enforcement authorities comply with the requirements of any guidance issued by the Agency to local authorities
- powers for the Agency to require local authorities to provide statistical returns and information on performance indicators
- powers to issue directions to local authorities
- powers for the Agency to undertake food surveillance and enforcement activity on its own behalf, or to direct another body to act on its behalf, either in partnership with or in

place of action by a local authority or local authorities
- powers for the Agency to take over enforcement activity from a local authority, or to reassign such work, when it considers such action to be in the national interest, or that an authority is failing to provide an adequate service
- powers for the Agency to recover from local authorities the cost, in whole or in part, of any work which it has taken over.

3.46 Further discussion with local authority representatives and other interested bodies, including public and consumer interests, will be required before the Government finalises proposals in this area. The discussions will also cover the future role of LACOTS in relation to food safety and standards. Where changes to the legal powers are thought to be desirable, specific proposals will be included in the draft Bill to be published during 1998, after consultation on this White Paper has been completed.

3.47 The Government accepts Professor James's recommendation that the Public Analyst Service in England and Wales, and the provision of scientific services for local authorities in Scotland, should be reviewed. The Minister of Agriculture, Fisheries and Food and the Secretary of State for Wales will initiate a review of the Public Analyst Service in England and Wales early this year, after the relationship of the Agency with local authorities has been clarified in the light of the discussions referred to above. A comprehensive review of the food-related scientific services in Scotland will be undertaken by a group representing all the main interests involved with an external chairperson. This review will be conducted in parallel with the review of the Public Analyst Service in England and Wales. It is also envisaged that a review will be carried out in Northern Ireland to ensure that the necessary laboratory services are available for food safety/standards purposes.

Chapter 4:
The Agency's Role in Food Safety

4.1 Food safety will be at the heart of the Agency's responsibilities. It will take a strategic view of food safety throughout the food chain and will be in a position to ensure that proper account is taken of the need to protect public health wherever Government action or inaction impinges on the safety of the food supply.

The Food Safety Act 1990

4.2 In Great Britain, the Food Safety Act 1990 prohibits the sale of food which is injurious to health, fails to comply with food safety requirements, is not of the nature, substance or quality demanded or is falsely described. It provides a due diligence defence for a defendant who can demonstrate that he did not cause the offence and had carried out all reasonable checks. The Act also provides for a wide range of regulations to be made in respect of many activities relating to food itself and also to food sources (live animals, growing crops) and contact materials (containers, packaging) so that the interests of consumers are protected and promoted. It provides for emergency control orders. It is proposed that the enabling powers will, after the establishment of the Agency, be used on the basis of the Agency's recommendations and that the subordinate legislation will be drafted by the Agency for Health Ministers.

4.3 Twenty Codes of Practice have been issued under the Food Safety Act to give guidance to food authorities on the execution and enforcement of the Act and Regulations and Orders made under it.

4.4 In Northern Ireland the Food Safety (Northern Ireland) Order 1991 and supporting regulations and codes of practice mirror the Food Safety Act provisions.

Food Safety on the Farm

4.5 It is essential for the Agency to be able to promote food safety throughout the whole of the food chain "from plough to plate". Food safety on the farm is, however, inextricably linked with other aspects of farming practices and policies, and the Government has therefore looked very closely at the existing Departmental responsibilities and legal controls with a view to defining precisely how the Agency's responsibilities should relate to those of other bodies, notably the Agriculture Departments, the Pesticides Safety Directorate (PSD) and the Veterinary Medicines Directorate (VMD). The Government considers that to give the Agency operational responsibility for all aspects of farming practices would risk diverting it from its essential aim of protecting public health. Moreover, it would, in practice, pass on to the Agency the same problems of conflicting objectives which have contributed to the decision to separate responsibility for the promotion of safe food from the Agriculture Ministers' responsibility for promoting the interests of the farming industry.

4.6 The Government's proposals are therefore designed to ensure that the Agency can intervene if it needs to where farming practices impact on the safety of food. It would normally achieve its objectives through participating fully and effectively in the formulation and implementation of Government policy on issues relating to farming practices where these impact on the safety of the human food chain. But, in addition, the Government proposes to ensure that the Agency is in a position to take action itself, should it consider it necessary to do so in the interests of protecting public health, if other mechanisms have failed. This action could take the form of directions to local authorities, exercising its own statutory enforcement powers, or recommending to Health Ministers that new subordinate legislation should be introduced under the Food Safety Act 1990.

4.7 The Government proposes to review the provisions of the Food Safety Act 1990 and to make any amendments necessary to provide the Agency with comprehensive powers to undertake surveillance and/or introduce control measures at all stages of the food chain, including on the farm. These powers would complement the provisions of other legislation in this area, in particular the Animal Health Act 1981, the Food and Environment Protection Act 1985 and the Agriculture Act 1970. The Agency will liaise closely with the Government Departments and other bodies with farm-related responsibilities to ensure that there is no unnecessary duplication of on-farm activities such as surveillance.

4.8   These proposals are consistent with Professor James's recommendation that the Agency's remit should cover the whole food chain, "from plough to plate". The Agency will participate in the management of all the food-related surveillance activities undertaken by Government and other bodies and will be able to initiate its own surveillance if it identifies gaps in the overall programme. Mechanisms are proposed to enable the Agency to help to ensure the effectiveness of the public protection policies of the Agriculture Departments and other bodies with responsibilities for on-farm activities. Most importantly, the Agency will be able itself to take action, for example by controlling the entry of food materials from the farm into the human food chain, if it considers that the actions taken by these other bodies do not provide a sufficient level of protection of public health. It will not, however, be distracted from its essential aims by taking on operational responsibility for policy areas where the primary focus is on matters other than public health (for example, environmental, economic or animal health and husbandry issues).

Surveillance and Control of Pathogens in Live Animals

4.9   Legal powers relevant to the surveillance and control of pathogenic agents in live animals are contained in the Animal Health Act 1981 (as amended), the Food Safety Act 1990 and the Food and Environment Protection Act 1985 (FEPA). In practice, the Animal Health Act powers have generally been used to introduce public or animal health measures relating to live animals on the

farm. For example, there are wide-ranging orders dealing with salmonella and BSE which cover public health as well as animal health requirements. The main on-farm use of the Food Safety Act powers has been in relation to the hygiene of on-farm milk production. The FEPA powers are used to make emergency orders in relation to any type of hazard which poses or may pose a risk to human health through food.

4.10   Hitherto policy on the control throughout the food chain of animal pathogens which may cause disease in humans has been fragmented. Creation of the Agency provides an opportunity to remedy this. The Government intends that the Agency should have a major strategic role in developing and implementing a national policy and strategy on the control of food-borne zoonoses throughout the food chain, working in close co-operation with Agriculture and Health Departments, public health professional bodies and the veterinary profession.

4.11   Food safety is frequently only one among a number of objectives for statutory measures dealing with animal disease. Other public health, animal health and welfare considerations and economic considerations may also be involved. The powers available to Agriculture Ministers under the Animal Health Act will therefore normally be the most effective vehicle for introducing statutory measures relating to live animals on the farm (and will be the only vehicle for dealing with zoonotic diseases which are transmitted through non-food routes). Agriculture Departments will work closely with the Agency in developing policy on on-farm surveillance and control of live animals. In order to facilitate close co-operation and to avoid duplication of on-farm activities:

- a joint Agency/Agriculture Departments Committee will be established to co-ordinate the surveillance programme; other interested bodies, including the PHLS, will participate in this Committee

- the Agency will be required to consult Agriculture Ministers on the option of using the Animal Health Act powers before recommending to Health Ministers that new measures should be introduced under the Food Safety Act. If the Agriculture Departments were unable or unwilling to use the Animal Health Act powers, the Agency could take the matter forward under the Food Safety Act provisions. Agriculture Departments would not be able to prevent the Agency from taking action.

4.12 BSE provides an illustration of how the arrangements will work in practice. The Agency will work closely with the Agriculture Departments on the control measures which are applied on-farm, and would be able to recommend to Health Ministers that supplementary measures should be introduced under the Food Safety Act if it considered that this was necessary to improve the protection offered to the public. The Agency would be free to publish this advice. Operationally the Agency will be responsible for developing and implementing BSE controls on the human food chain from the slaughterhouse onwards, and Agriculture Ministers will be responsible for the eradication of the disease from the national cattle herd, including controls on rendering plants, and for measures aimed at securing the lifting of the EC ban on exports of British beef.

4.13 The Spongiform Encephalopathy Advisory Committee (SEAC), which advises Government on all matters relating to BSE and CJD, will advise the Agency in the same way as it currently advises Agriculture and Health Departments on the food safety implications of BSE. The Agency will be consulted on appointments to SEAC and will participate, with MAFF and the Department of Health, in the secretariat.

Animal Feedingstuffs

4.14 Animal feedingstuffs form an important part of the food chain and have implications for the safety and quality of the food which is supplied to the consumer. The Government considers it necessary for the Agency to have powers in relation to animal feedingstuffs in order to exercise effectively its responsibility to safeguard human health across the whole food chain. The composition and safety of animal feeds also has an important impact however on animal health and husbandry.

4.15 There is currently a range of legal controls under the Agriculture Act 1970 and the European Communities Act 1972 governing the safety, composition and labelling of animal feedingstuffs. Most of these implement EC Directives. For example, there are controls on additives in feedingstuffs which provide a positive list of substances approved against criteria of safety (for consumers, animals and operators), quality and efficacy; permitted levels of contaminants; and rules on the composition and labelling of feedingstuffs, which include a negative list of prohibited ingredients compiled on grounds of protecting human and animal health. There are currently no controls specifically covering the use of genetically modified materials in animal feed, which are considered on a case-by-case basis, though EC proposals are expected shortly.

4.16 Important controls have been put in place under the Animal Health Act 1981 to prohibit the feeding of mammalian protein to ruminants and mammalian meat and bonemeal to any livestock. These are the key controls to prevent the spread of BSE in animals. In addition, there are requirements on the standards to which animal by-products for use in animal feeds must be processed and the microbiological standards which the processed products must meet.

4.17 The Government recognises that animal feedingstuffs is an area where there is both a public health interest and an animal health and husbandry interest. It believes that the creation of the Food Standards Agency offers an opportunity to improve the co-ordination of work on animal feedingstuffs, to ensure that full account is taken of the public health considerations. In 1992, an expert group on animal feedingstuffs chaired by Professor Eric Lamming recommended that an independent advisory committee on animal feedingstuffs should be created to consider those issues relating to animal feed not falling within the remit of other expert advisory committees. This recommendation has not been implemented. The present Government believes that the need for such an advisory committee has now become pressing, particularly in the light of public concerns about the use of genetically modified feed ingredients such as genetically modified maize. It therefore proposes to implement the recommendation of the Lamming Committee to create an independent Advisory Committee on Animal Feedingstuffs.

4.18 This Committee would advise on all matters not covered by existing Advisory Committees affecting the safety, quality and efficacy of animal feeds, including the implications for human health: for example the content of animal feedingstuffs; animal nutrition; the assessment of new animal feeds and feeding practices including genetically modified products; and advice on the line to take on negotiating and implementing EC measures. Its membership would include expertise in microbiology, toxicology, veterinary medicine, biotechnology and human health as well as the interests of consumers, and enforcement authorities. The Committee would be appointed jointly by the Agency and Agriculture Ministers, who would share its secretariat.

4.19 The Government proposes that responsibility for animal feedingstuffs matters should be divided between the Agency and Agriculture Departments. The Agency will take the lead on those issues where there are close links with the arrangements for human food, for example:

- the use of genetically modified ingredients in feedingstuffs
- feed additives
- composition and labelling of feedingstuffs
- contaminants in feedingstuffs.

4.20 The Agency will also co-ordinate and audit local authority enforcement activities in these areas.

4.21 The Agency will, as proposed in paragraph 4.7 above, have powers to initiate surveillance of animal feedingstuffs. Powers already exist under the Food Safety Act 1990 to respond to any emergency affecting food safety, including problems originating in animal feedingstuffs. The Agency will have responsibility for operating these powers.

4.22 The Agency will need to liaise very closely with Agriculture Departments, which would retain operational responsibilities for controls on the use of mammalian protein in feedingstuffs which are key measures preventing the spread of BSE in animals; and the provisions relating to the use of animal by-products in animal feeds and other animal health measures such as rules for the treatment of swill for feeding to pigs which are designed to control classical swine fever. These measures can most efficiently continue to be operated by the State Veterinary Service, working in close liaison with the Agency. If the Agency believes there are significant gaps in the protection provided to human health by the Agriculture Departments' exercise of these responsibilities, it will be able to make public its views and to make use of its own powers under the Food Safety Act to ensure that any necessary work was undertaken.

Pesticides and veterinary medicines

4.23 Legal controls on pesticides are laid down in the Control of Pesticides Regulations 1986, the Control of Substances Hazardous to Health

Regulations 1994 and the Pesticides (Maximum Residue Levels in Crops, Food and Feedingstuffs) Regulations 1994. European law, designed to harmonise authorisation arrangements for plant protection products, also applies in the area. Responsibility for pesticide approvals in the UK rests with the Ministry of Agriculture, Fisheries and Food, the Department of Health, the Department of the Environment, Transport and the Regions and the Scottish, Welsh and Northern Ireland Offices. Ministers are advised on the use of pesticides, the assessment of applications and the review of existing products by the independent Advisory Committee on Pesticides (ACP). One official from each of the responsible Departments acts as an Assessor to the ACP. Assessors are responsible for "signing off" authorisations; that is granting or refusing agreement to the recommendations of the Committee on behalf of Departmental Ministers. The unanimous agreement of Assessors is needed in order for an application to be granted. The approvals system is administered in Great Britain by the Pesticides Safety Directorate (PSD), an Executive Agency of MAFF, for most pesticides including horticultural, agricultural and amateur garden products, and the Health and Safety Executive (HSE), for other non-agricultural pesticides.

4.24 Arrangements for the authorisation of veterinary medicines are harmonised across the Community under EC law, which also controls manufacture and wholesale dealing, sets maximum residue limits for a range of products and includes requirements for residues surveillance. EC law also provides the basis for the approval of zootechnical feed additives, and will shortly be extended to require the authorisation of the individual products containing them (which is currently carried out in the UK under the Medicines Act 1968). Post-licensing monitoring of suspected adverse reactions (SARs) to veterinary medicines is required both by EC legislation and the Medicines Act 1968. Surveillance of residues and veterinary medicines in meat and other animal products is required

under both EC legislation and the Food Safety Act. Responsibility for veterinary medicines matters in the United Kingdom rests with the Minister of Agriculture, Fisheries and Food, the Secretary of State for Health and the other Agriculture and Health Ministers, who jointly form the Licensing Authority. The issue of marketing authorisations, controls on manufacture and distribution of veterinary medicinal products, surveillance programmes and policy advice on those matters to the Licensing Authority are delegated to the Veterinary Medicines Directorate (VMD), an Executive Agency of MAFF. Ministers are advised on veterinary medicines applications by the independent Veterinary Products Committee (VPC).

4.25 Professor James's recommendation that responsibility for the food safety evaluation of pesticides and veterinary medicines should transfer to the Agency resulted in a substantial volume of comment in the consultation exercise. Although there was broad agreement that the Agency should have a locus in this area, doubts were expressed about the practicality of implementing his proposals. The food safety evaluation of pesticides and veterinary medicines is part of an integrated process which is designed not only to protect the consumer but to safeguard the user of the product, neighbours and bystanders, the environment and — for veterinary medicines — the target animal as well. Moreover, safety evaluation is linked to efficacy, and the two cannot readily be separated. It was widely felt that an approach which dismantled these arrangements risked weakening the evaluation process as a whole, and that product safety might be compromised as a result.

4.26 There is also a substantial European dimension to the work, particularly for veterinary medicines. It was suggested that those wanting access to UK markets would take alternative routes, either seeking authorisation from VMD's competitors overseas and applying for authorisation here under "mutual recognition" arrangements, or seeking authorisation from the European Agency for the Evaluation of Medicinal Products for a licence valid in all Member States. This would seriously weaken the UK's ability to influence European approvals of veterinary products and therefore the protection of food safety. Although the EC regime for agricultural pesticides is less advanced, similar concerns apply.

4.27 The Government considers that, in view of the above arguments, the objectives of Professor James's recommendations can best be met by introducing an extensive range of mechanisms and safeguards to provide the Agency with a powerful and effective input into the public safety aspects of the work of PSD and VMD and with the powers to veto products should this be necessary for public health reasons. However, the Government believes that to ensure effective evaluation and clearance of pesticides and veterinary medicines the public safety aspects of the work should be kept together with the other aspects of the evaluation process, and that, subject to the arrangements described below, PSD and VMD should continue to be Executive Agencies of MAFF and should retain lead operational responsibility for authorisations.

4.28 The Government proposes to introduce the following mechanisms to enable the Agency to ensure that proper account is taken of food safety considerations in the authorisation of pesticides and the licensing of veterinary medicines.

4.29 The Agency will:

- provide assessors/advisors to the Advisory Committee on Pesticides and the Veterinary Products Committee and their subcommittees. These assessors' duty to "sign off" authorisations for pesticides would give the Agency an effective veto. There would be similar but less formal powers in relation to veterinary medicines. As an additional safeguard in the case of

veterinary medicines, the Health Ministers, as members of the Licensing Authority, could block an application if they considered on the basis of advice from the Agency that the product posed an unacceptable risk
- nominate a member to the independent ACP and VPC, which formulate advice to Ministers on individual authorisations
- be consulted on membership of the ACP and VPC as a whole
- provide a scientific liaison officer to the ACP and VPC, who would have a scientific input to papers, help set the agenda for meetings and be involved in the briefing process
- have access to information on human Suspected Adverse Reactions (SARs) to veterinary medicines through its representation on the VPC, against the possibility that SARs to residues in food becomes an issue in future
- provide a member of the ownership boards for PSD and VMD to ensure that it is fully represented when advice for Ministers is prepared
- work closely with PSD and VMD on drawing up their surveillance programmes; provide a member of the Working Party on Pesticide Residues and of the Advisory Group on Veterinary Residues and be consulted on the appointment of the Chairpersons of these committees
- have powers under the Food Safety Act to carry out its own surveillance for residues of pesticides and veterinary medicines in food, should it consider it necessary to supplement the PSD/VMD programmes
- provide advice on EU and other international discussions.

4.30 The Government considers that the Agency should have a clear input into policy-making for all areas which affect human health in relation to food. The Agency will:

- be a statutory consultee on the public health implications of PSD's and VMD's policy advice
- provide advice on EU and other international discussions relating to the use of pesticides and veterinary medicines insofar as it relates to food.

4.31 However, as the development of policy on the use of pesticides and veterinary medicines has implications which extend far beyond questions of food safety, the Government proposes that this responsibility should remain with PSD and VMD respectively.

4.32 As in other areas, the Agency would be able to make public any concerns it had about the Government's decisions and actions on pesticides and veterinary medicines. This freedom to publish its views will give it considerable influence in its dealings with PSD and VMD.

Food Hygiene

4.33 The effect of the Food Safety Act's provisions is to put the onus on food businesses to produce safe food. The general provisions of the Food Safety Act are supplemented by specific hygiene requirements which are largely derived from EC legislation. Council Directive 93/43/EEC on the Hygiene of Foodstuffs (the "horizontal" Directive) applies to food caterers and food retailers and to the manufacture, handling etc of products of non-animal origin. In addition there are 14 hygiene Directives (the "vertical" Directives) covering animal products. These Directives generally apply to processors and wholesalers, but not at the retail and catering stages of the distribution chain. The Directives are implemented in national legislation in the UK by means of Regulations made under the Food Safety Act 1990.

4.34 The European Commission is undertaking a major public consultation with a view to consolidating and simplifying the product-specific hygiene legislation. The intention is to extend the hazard analysis approach to food safety controls across the board and to group common provisions, but to retain prescriptive requirements where necessary to address risks specific to individual product types or sectors.

4.35 The Advisory Committee on the Microbiological Safety of Food (ACMSF) was established in 1990 to provide independent expert advice to UK Health and Agriculture Ministers on matters related to the microbiological safety of food, and to inform the policy and decision making processes.

4.36 The Agency will:

- take over Health and Agriculture Departments' responsibility for advising Ministers on all aspects of food hygiene policy and policy on the microbiological safety of food
- initiate any legislative action or other activity which might be required to protect public health, for example in promoting the use of HACCP (Hazard Analysis and Critical Control Points)
- become the UK central competent authority for the EC hygiene Directives (day-to-day responsibility for enforcement would remain with local authorities or the Meat Hygiene Service or the Dairy Hygiene Inspectorate as at present)
- play a proactive role in the development of EC policy and legislation on food hygiene
- represent the UK in international negotiations on food hygiene matters
- commission research and surveillance relating to food hygiene and microbiological safety, and co-ordinate research and surveillance carried out by other bodies (such as PHLS and MAFF and its Agencies) which has a bearing on food safety
- provide the secretariat of the ACMSF

- provide advice, information and guidance to consumers, industry and enforcement authorities.

Meat and Milk Hygiene

4.37 Meat and milk hygiene legislation, like other food hygiene legislation, is largely based on EC Directives. Fresh meat plants are licensed by the Agriculture Departments. Meat inspection and enforcement of the hygiene legislation (including the specified risk material legislation which lays down requirements designed to prevent the transmission of the BSE agent to humans) in licensed plants are carried out by the Meat Hygiene Service (MHS — an Executive Agency of MAFF) in Great Britain on behalf of the Minister of Agriculture and the Secretaries of State for Scotland and for Wales. Some slaughterhouses fall outside the scope of the licensing requirements; local authorities are responsible for enforcement in these premises. In Northern Ireland responsibility is shared between the Department of Agriculture for Northern Ireland (DANI) and local authorities.

4.38 In England and Wales the Minister of Agriculture and Secretary of State for Wales are responsible for registering and inspecting dairy holdings to ensure compliance with the Dairy Products (Hygiene) Regulations 1995 and for the microbiological testing of milk which is sold untreated. This work is carried out by the Dairy Hygiene Inspectorate of the Farming and Rural Conservation Agency, an Executive Agency of MAFF and the Welsh Office which was set up in 1997 to carry out the non-privatisable functions of ADAS. In Scotland all dairy hygiene work is the responsibility of local authorities, and in Northern Ireland DANI is responsible.

4.39 Professor James recommended that the recently established Meat Hygiene Service should not be dismantled, but that the Agency should take over responsibility for the MHS and the dairy hygiene responsibilities of the Minister of Agriculture and Secretary of State for Wales. The Government agrees that the MHS should report in future to the Agency rather than to Agriculture Ministers. It also agrees that the Agency should take over the MAFF/Welsh Office dairy hygiene responsibilities. All dairy hygiene work in Scotland will remain the responsibility of local authorities.

4.40 In addition to the activities listed in 4.36 above, the Agency will:

- take over responsibility for formulating policy and advising on legislation on (i) hygiene standards in all types of meat plants and (ii) meat inspection charges
- take over responsibility for formulating policy and advising on legislation designed to prevent the transmission of the BSE agent through the human food chain. (The relationship between the Agency and the Spongiform Encephalopathy Advisory Committee (SEAC) is discussed in paragraph 4.13)
- take over the Agriculture Ministers' responsibilities for licensing fresh meat plants and for approvals of meat products and meat preparations plants which are co-located with fresh meat plants. (Approval of other meat products and meat preparations plants will remain the responsibility of the local authority)
- as "owner" of the MHS, set and publish its performance targets and monitor its performance against these targets. (The Agency's territorial Executives in Scotland and Wales (see Chapter 7) would be responsible for setting targets for and monitoring the MHS's activities in Scotland and Wales)
- maintain and update the Operations Manual of the MHS. The Agency will consult and agree instructions and procedures with MAFF on issues which are relevant to animal health and international trade in animal products (which are the responsibility of the Chief Veterinary Officer (CVO))

- publish a regular BSE Enforcement Bulletin and a Meat Hygiene Enforcement Report
- take over the responsibilities of the Minister of Agriculture and the Secretary of State for Wales for dairy hygiene enforcement work. The Government envisages that, initially at least, the Agency will continue to discharge these responsibilities through the Farming and Rural Conservation Agency
- discharge meat and dairy hygiene responsibilities in Northern Ireland through arrangements with DANI. These arrangements will be set out in an agreement which describes the relationship between the Agency and DANI and provides for the Agency to audit the performance of these responsibilities.

4.41 The State Veterinary Service (SVS) currently audits the enforcement of the specified risk material legislation by visiting all relevant premises on a monthly basis. This audit — which is carried out for both public and animal health purposes — is expected to continue. The Agency and the SVS will need to agree the procedures for the audit. The Agency will have powers to take follow-up action in premises producing food should this be necessary.

4.42 The Chief Veterinary Officer is responsible for ensuring that animal products traded on the European Single Market or internationally, comply with the appropriate animal and public health requirements. In order to discharge this responsibility he needs to audit the MHS's functions in relation to the application of the EC health mark to meat, meat products, meat preparations and minced meat produced in accordance with EC Directives, and the veterinary certification which the MHS provides to meet the requirements of importing third countries. It is expected that the Agency's Veterinary Public Health Unit, which will monitor the MHS's performance as described in paragraph 4.40 above, will also carry out any

veterinary audit which the CVO requires, in accordance with arrangements to be agreed between the Agency and MAFF.

4.43 Agriculture Departments will remain responsible for legislation relating to the welfare of animals at slaughter. However, to avoid duplication of effort, the Agency through the Meat Hygiene Service will carry out enforcement on behalf of the Agriculture Departments in those premises where the MHS is responsible for enforcement of the hygiene legislation.

Food-borne Illness

4.44 Professor James recommended that responsibility for dealing with outbreaks of food-borne illness should remain with local authorities and health authorities, assisted by the Public Health Laboratory Service (PHLS), but that the Agency should be conjointly responsible and should have reserve powers of audit and enforcement. He also suggested that the PHLS should report directly to the Agency, from which it would receive funds for its food-related work.

4.45 The Government agrees that local investigations should continue to be managed at local level. Investigations should continue to be led by the relevant health authority's Consultant in Communicable Disease Control (CCDC) (Consultant in Public Health Medicine — CPHM — in Scotland) and the local authority. Much of the work will be carried out by local authority staff. The existing arrangements for outbreak management involve all those with the necessary information and expertise and provide a sound foundation on which to build. The Agency's role generally should be supportive rather than operational, except where an incident requires management beyond the local level or where the responsible authorities at local level fail to manage an incident successfully. Where food is identified as a source of an outbreak, and the scale or severity of the hazard warrants central involvement, the Agency will have responsibility for the management of the Food Hazard Warning System, and for liaison with the Chief Medical Officers in England, Wales, Scotland and Northern Ireland to whom major outbreaks would continue to be reported.

4.46 The legislative basis for these arrangements is the Public Health (Control of Disease) Act 1984 in England and Wales; the Public Health (Scotland) Act 1897; the Food Safety Act 1990 in Great Britain; the Public Health Act (Northern Ireland) 1967 and the Food Safety (Northern Ireland) Order 1991; and their associated regulations. In considering Professor James's recommendations, the Government has identified two areas where the current legislative controls may need to be strengthened. The Government has already announced that it will be consulting on proposals for revising and streamlining legislation on control of communicable diseases, to replace the Public Health (Control of Disease) Act 1984; a review of the corresponding legislation will also be undertaken in Scotland. One issue which this raises is whether the arrangements for statutory notification of diseases should be extended to include reporting by clinical laboratories of certain specified (human) test results. The Government also proposes to strengthen the Food Safety Act surveillance powers to ensure that surveillance can be undertaken across the whole of the food chain without requiring the consent of the businesses which are to be surveyed. The Government intends that the Northern Ireland legislation will continue to remain in step with that in Great Britain. The Agency will play a major role in co-ordinating surveillance, and will work with those currently engaged in such activities and with the UK Health and Agriculture Departments.

4.47 The Government agrees that it will be particularly important to establish a clear relationship between the Agency and the PHLS and to set this out in a service level agreement. This will recognise that the PHLS provides a unique service combining expertise in the microbiological safety of food and food-borne illness with expertise in epidemiology at both central and local levels in a national organisation, and which must continue to cover both food-borne and other human diseases in an integrated way (some diseases can be transmitted both through food and in other ways — for example person to person). The relationship between the Agency and PHLS will also clearly recognise the strategic role of the Agency in co-ordinating surveillance activity throughout the food chain. (See paragraphs 4.7 and 4.8 above).

4.48 In view of the integrated nature of PHLS's work, the Government does not propose to route part of the PHLS's core funding through the Agency. It is not possible separately to identify "food" and "non-food" functions within PHLS's national surveillance; and priorities for the PHLS's local work in support of Environmental Health Departments (EHDs) should continue to be set by these EHD customers to reflect local needs. However, the Department of Health's central budget for surveillance and research projects related to food-borne illness, which is used to commission work from PHLS and others, should transfer to the Agency; and the arrangements for funding the surveys which PHLS currently carries out in conjunction with LACOTS should be settled in the light of decisions on the future role of LACOTS (see paragraph 3.46).

4.49 To reinforce the Agency's status as a key customer of the PHLS, the Department of Health will invite it to customer liaison meetings and relevant in-year reviews relating to the food work of the PHLS; and will consult it, as of right, before the annual Ministerial Accountability Review of the PHLS.

Scotland and Northern Ireland

4.50 Professor James recognised that there was no PHLS in Scotland and acknowledged the role of the Scottish Centre for Infection and Environmental Health (SCIEH) and the network of laboratories that report to it. The Agency will have a similar relationship with SCIEH to that proposed with the PHLS. The Government has already agreed that there will be a review of food-related laboratory services in Scotland; the nature of the contracting and funding arrangements for the comprehensive surveillance system that will be required by the Agency will be determined in the light of that review.

4.51 In Northern Ireland, the Public Health Laboratory (PHL) at Belfast City Hospital provides public health microbiological services covering food, water and environmental aspects. Currently, the regional surveillance function is carried out by the Department of Health and Social Services for Northern Ireland. Considerations similar to those impacting on the PHLS will apply in relation to the PHL in Northern Ireland.

4.52 The Agency will:

- identify and set standards, drawing on appropriate expert advice, for good management of local investigations (eg conduct of enquiries, use of surveillance, and communications with the public) and will audit against these standards
- take a strategic view of human and animal surveillance, in co-ordination with the Health and Agriculture Departments, PHLS, SCIEH and other Agencies, and of research and development
- co-ordinate and commission food surveillance programmes
- help local authorities and health authorities (health boards in Scotland) to overcome local boundaries, through supportive intervention where appropriate, in the investigation of food hazards and food-borne outbreaks
- establish a service level agreement with the PHLS in England and Wales
- take over responsibility from the Health Departments for the Food Hazard Warning System and liaise with the relevant Chief Medical Officers in respect of major outbreaks

- be given default powers to allow it to step in where local management of an outbreak is not effective.

Novel foods and processes

4.53 All novel foods, including genetically modified (GM) foods, are regulated by the EC Novel Foods Regulation (258/97) which replaces the previous voluntary approval system which operated in the UK from the early 1980s. The independent Advisory Committee on Novel Foods and Processes (ACNFP) provides advice on the assessment of novel food applications. Other Advisory Committees may also be asked for advice. In considering the environmental impact of any genetically modified organisms (GMOs) intended for food, advice will be obtained from the Department of the Environment, Transport and the Regions (DETR) and the Advisory Committee on Releases to the Environment (ACRE). Under the Genetically Modified Organisms (Deliberate Release) Regulations 1992 (as amended) the Minister of Agriculture, Fisheries and Food in England acts jointly with the Secretary of State for the Environment on matters in which he has an interest and consents are issued on their behalf by DETR. In Scotland or Wales consents are issued on behalf of the Secretary of State for Scotland or Wales as appropriate. Parallel legislation is in place for Northern Ireland.

4.54 The EC Novel Foods Regulation does not cover food irradiation, which is the subject of a draft EC Directive which is currently under consideration by the European Parliament. In the UK food irradiation is controlled by the Food (Control of Irradiation) Regulations 1990. In accordance with these regulations food irradiation facilities must be licensed and inspected.

4.55 The Agency will:

- become the UK competent authority for assessing novel food applications in accordance with the requirements of the

EC Novel Foods Regulation, drawing on advice from ACNFP and other UK and European Advisory Committees as necessary

- be responsible for licensing and inspecting food irradiation facilities under the 1990 Regulations
- take over the Agriculture Ministers' responsibilities for issuing consents under the Deliberate Release Regulations for GMOs intended for food and animal feed
- provide the secretariat to ACNFP
- develop and implement future policy on the control of novel foods and processes and play a proactive role in the development of EC controls
- play an active role in moves towards international harmonisation of safety assessment procedures for novel foods
- commission research to underpin safety assessment of novel foods
- provide information and advice to consumers, enforcement authorities, Government Departments and industry.

Food Additives

4.56 All the major classes of food additives are now controlled through EC Directives. The Agency will take over the responsibilities of Agriculture and Health Departments in the UK for all food additives matters, including negotiations in the EU. In particular it will:

- initiate any action, including regulatory action, which might be required to protect public health in the light of new information about the safety or use of food additives
- monitor the use of food additives and take appropriate steps to ensure that the intake of food additives does not exceed recommended levels
- process applications for temporary national authorisation of new food additives, as provided for in EC legislation

- develop improved methods for assessing the safety of food additives and monitoring intakes
- commission research to support the above activities
- provide information and advice to consumers, enforcement authorities, Government Departments and industry
- provide the Secretariat to the Food Advisory Committee (whose remit includes, but goes much wider than, food additives).

4.57 In exercising these functions the Agency will draw as necessary on the advice of the independent Advisory Committees at both national and European level.

Chemical contaminants in food

4.58 Detailed regulations control the presence in food of several chemical contaminants including arsenic, lead, tin and aflatoxins. The European Commission is in the process of harmonising controls on contaminants across the EU and the first Commission regulation, which sets maximum limits for nitrate in lettuce and spinach, has been adopted. Other proposals, on aflatoxins and the heavy metals lead and cadmium, are under discussion. Food contact materials and articles, which include food packaging, are controlled by EC Framework Directive 89/109 and a series of specific Directives covering plastics, vinyl chloride, ceramics and regenerated cellulose film. All of these have been implemented in the UK. The basic principle of these Directives is that food contact materials should not transfer their constituent chemicals into food so as to harm health. The Agency will take over the responsibilities of Agriculture and Health Departments in the UK for all matters concerning chemical contaminants in food (which include natural toxicants, inorganic and organic environmental contaminants and chemicals migrating from materials and articles in contact with food).

4.59 The Agency will:

- plan, carry out and report the results of surveys to establish dietary intakes from food and the extent of contamination by specific chemicals in the food supply
- develop and implement future policy on chemical contaminants in food and play a proactive role in the development of EC controls and in negotiations in other fora (eg Codex)
- commission research to support the safety assessment of food chemical contaminants and inform policy formulation
- provide information and advice to consumers, industry (including primary producers e.g. on natural toxicants) enforcement authorities, and Government Departments
- act as a statutory consultee for Integrated Pollution Control applications to determine whether requested discharges from industrial plants might cause adverse effects on the food chain.

4.60 The Government is considering whether any further powers may be needed to enable the Agency to fulfil its responsibility to protect the safety of the food chain.

Radiological safety

4.61 Discharges of radioactive waste and other sources of radioactivity are controlled under the Radioactive Substances Act 1993. At present the Environment Agency is responsible for authorising discharges in England and Wales; the Minister of Agriculture and the Secretary of State for Wales are statutory consultees and may direct the Environment Agency and call in applications for authorisations for determination. The Minister and the Secretary of State for Wales also have an appellate function. In Scotland, the Scottish Environmental Protection Agency (SEPA) is responsible for authorising discharges and the Secretary of State for Scotland is a statutory

consultee. The Secretary of State has a general power to give directions to SEPA and also has power to call in applications for his own determination. Decisions taken by SEPA in this area are also subject to appeal to the Secretary of State. In Northern Ireland the Chief Radiochemical Inspector of the Environment and Heritage Services is responsible for the authorisation of discharges.

4.62 Under the terms of the Radiological Protection Act 1970, the National Radiological Protection Board undertakes research and provides information and advice about the protection of people from radiation hazards. The Agency will be able to call on its advice.

4.63 The Agency will:

- develop and maintain methodology for the assessment of the impact of discharges of radioactive waste and other sources of radioactivity in the food supply
- become the statutory consultee of the Environment Agency and SEPA on the radiological impact of discharges in relation to proposed discharge limits in applications for authorisations
- develop and maintain a surveillance programme for radioactivity in the food chain, and co-ordinate its surveillance activities with the Environment Agency and others carrying out radiological surveillance
- provide information and advice to consumers, industry, enforcement authorities and Government Departments.

4.64 The Secretary of State for Health will acquire the Minister of Agriculture's powers to direct the Environment Agency and call in applications for authorisations for determination. The Government is considering whether any further powers may be needed to enable the Agency to fulfil its responsibility to protect the safety of the food chain.

Food intolerance

4.65 Food intolerance is a general term used to describe any untoward reaction to food experienced by individuals. It includes reactions resulting from a variety of different mechanisms and includes food allergy (a specific reaction involving the immune system) and behavioural effects which may be caused by food. The main areas of concern from the public health standpoint are food allergies which in some cases can be severe and may even be life threatening.

4.66 The Agency will:

- provide information, guidance and advice to industry, caterers and the public
- develop and negotiate for changes to EC labelling rules to inform the public on possible risks from allergens
- commission research to improve scientific understanding of the problem
- consider the need for surveillance studies to assess the prevalence of allergic reactions to foods, including novel foods.

Food Emergencies

4.67 Food emergencies occur when circumstances exist which are likely to create a hazard to human health through human consumption of contaminated food. In such circumstances it is necessary to evaluate the potential risk to human health and take whatever action is necessary to protect the public. This may include the provision of advice to the public, the food industry and farmers, the use of voluntary agreements with farmers or traders to withhold contaminated produce, or emergency legislation under the Food Safety Act or the Food and Environment Protection Act 1985.

4.68 The Agency will:

- liaise with Government Departments and their executive agencies at a national and local level, with the Scottish Executive and the Welsh Assembly and with local authorities, to ensure a co-ordinated response
- prepare plans for emergencies and incidents involving the contamination of food or the food chain with toxic chemical or radioactive materials
- organise regular exercises simulating major emergencies and participate in nuclear operators' and overseas emergency exercises
- continue the existing monitoring programme on post-Chernobyl issues
- commission research to enhance its ability to respond effectively to emergencies.

Water

4.69 The Agency will have responsibility for those aspects of water quality which fall within the Food Safety Act, namely the safety, composition and labelling of bottled water, and the safety of all water sold or used by food businesses once it has left the supply. However, broader responsibility for the supply of wholesome water will remain the responsibility of the Secretaries of State for Environment, Transport and the Regions and for Wales, Scotland and Northern Ireland. The Water Industry Act 1991, the Water (Scotland) Act 1980 and the Water and Sewerage Services (Northern Ireland) Order 1973, as amended, set the legal requirements for drinking water which will continue to be enforced by the Drinking Water Inspectorate (DWI) for England and Wales; the Agriculture, Environment and Fisheries Department of the Scottish Office; and the Drinking Water Inspectorate of the Environment and Heritage Service Agency, Northern Ireland. The Agency will wish to establish good relations and exchange information with the DETR and the DWI and the parallel bodies in Scotland and Northern Ireland on matters affecting drinking water.

Other Areas

4.70 The Government does not consider it appropriate to give the Agency responsibility for subjects such as animal welfare or environmental policy where the primary focus of activity relates to issues other than food safety and standards. It would, however, be open to the Agency, as an independent body, to make public its views on the food safety implications of issues outside its own remit, and so to exercise a significant influence on Government policy in these areas.

Chapter 5:
The Agency's Role in Food Standards and Nutrition

5.1 People need to be given clear and authoritative information about food in order to make informed choices about their own diet. The Agency's proposed responsibilities in the areas of food standards and nutrition will enable it to ensure that this information is provided.

Food Standards

5.2 Food standards encompasses compositional standards, labelling requirements and food authenticity. The legal framework on compositional standards and labelling of foodstuffs is now almost entirely derived from EC legislation.

5.3 The proposal that the Agency should take over responsibility for this important area extends its remit beyond food safety to include matters concerned with food quality, consumer protection and choice. Consumers have a right to be properly informed about the content and compositional quality of the food they purchase, and to be confident that they will not be misled as a result of inadequate, inaccurate or fraudulent information given by producers, manufacturers or retailers. The quality of information provided also has implications for the safety of individual consumers: for example, individuals who suffer from severe allergies.

5.4 Compliance with standards of composition and labelling is also important to ensure fair conditions of trade in the Single European Market and the world market for food. Consumers and UK industry may be disadvantaged and choice reduced if inconsistent or over-restrictive standards create barriers to trade. The Agency will therefore need to work closely with industry as well as with consumers in taking forward policy development in this area.

5.5 The Agency will:

- be responsible for policy and legislation on compositional standards of foodstuffs

- be responsible for policy and legislation on the labelling of food at retail and catering level, including for example ingredient listing, nutrition labelling and claims
- undertake surveillance programmes on food authenticity to ensure consumers are not misled, in co-ordination with enforcement authorities
- play a proactive role in developing EC controls on claims relating to nutrition and health
- develop a close working relationship with the Medicines Control Agency on the borderline between food and medicinal products
- establish close working relationships with DTI on general consumer protection matters, weights and measures legislation and other relevant issues
- advise MAFF on labelling and other food standards issues which arise in the context of Common Agricultural Policy (CAP) regimes on individual commodities (for example, definition of alcoholic drinks, water content of frozen poultry meat, marketing standards for eggs etc), or other EC requirements, for example measures relating to food marketing.

Nutrition

5.6 The recommendation in the James Report that the Agency should develop policy, issue guidance and propose legislation on the nutritional quality of diets and their effect on public health provoked considerable comment during the consultation exercise. Responses from consumer organisations, academics and public health organisations and professionals were overwhelmingly in favour of including nutrition in the remit of the Agency. Many respondents from the food and farming industries (but not all) considered that the inclusion of nutrition might detract from the Agency's clarity of purpose and effectiveness in improving microbiological and chemical safety standards.

5.7 "Nutrition" is not a single term. It encompasses a wide range of functions from the nutrient content of food to advice about healthy eating. These elements will be assigned between the Agency and the Health Departments on the basis of the following criteria:

- functions relating to the information which the public needs about food will go to the Agency
- public health functions, such as the links between diet and health, will remain with the Department of Health; and
- the interface between the two will be a shared responsibility.

5.8 This means that, while the Agency will provide readily intelligible, scientifically-based advice about the nutritional content of foods, it will not tell people what they should eat. Instead it will concentrate its efforts on its core functions of ensuring the *safety* of what people eat and providing authoritative and unbiased information to help people decide for themselves what they wish to eat. The Health Departments will retain responsibility for wider public health policy, including behavioural and lifestyle issues where nutrition is an important factor.

5.9 The overlapping functions fall in the area covered by the work of the Advisory Committee on Medical Aspects of Food and Nutrition Policy (COMA), which provides advice to Ministers on the risks associated with people's diets. COMA will therefore be serviced jointly by the Agency and Department of Health. This arrangement will ensure that the Agency is fully involved in COMA's work, and will avoid the risk that the Agency and Health Departments might become regarded as separate sources of advice on what constitutes a healthy diet.

5.10 The area of nutrition has been the subject of vigorous debate since the James Report was published and the Government expects that these proposals will attract detailed comments, in particular on the attribution of responsibility proposed in paragraphs 5.11, 5.12 and 5.13 below. In particular the Government expects that there will continue to be debate on whether the responsibility for definition of a balanced, healthy diet should rest with the Agency, with Health Departments or with the Agency and Health Departments jointly, and will welcome further comments on this issue. It will consider the precise attribution of responsibilities further in the light of the response to this White Paper.

5.11 The Government proposes that the Agency will:

- be responsible for monitoring and surveillance of the nutrient content of food and the nutrient content of the diet
- provide authoritative factual information about the nutrient content of individual foods and advice on the diet as a whole
- secure expert scientific advice on the relationship between diet, nutritional status and health to support the definition of a healthy diet and to inform policy from the Committee on Medical Aspects of Food and Nutrition Policy (COMA)
- provide the definition of a balanced diet, based on COMA's scientific advice, for subsequent use in health education material produced by other bodies
- where appropriate, propose legislation relating to nutritional aspects of food, including labelling and claims, dietary supplements sold as food, fortified foods and functional foods
- provide practical guidance in relation to nutritional aspects of the food chain, including production and catering
- commission food and diet research appropriate to the functions of the Agency
- represent the UK in international negotiations on issues relating to nutritional aspects of food

● formulate policy and provide advice to Ministers on these issues.

5.12 The Agency will share with Health Departments responsibility for:

● providing the joint secretariat to the Committee on Medical Aspects of Food and Nutrition Policy (COMA). (COMA will advise Health Departments and the Agency)
● surveillance of the nutritional status of people
● defining the health education message on nutritional issues, taking account of both food and wider health issues
● policy formulation and advice to Ministers on these issues, for example in relation to Our Healthier Nation, and public health aspects of food fortification.

5.13 Health Departments will retain responsibility for:

● wider public health policy issues including conditions (such as cardiovascular disease, cancer, osteoporosis or obesity) where nutritional status is one of a number of risk factors
● consideration of vulnerable groups and inequalities issues
● health education on wider behavioural issues which may include but go beyond nutrition (such as smoking, drinking, physical activity)
● all links with the NHS and health professionals, breastfeeding promotion in the NHS, clinical nutrition and dietetics including hospital catering and nutritional therapy
● dietary supplements which are controlled by the Medicines Act (through the Medicines Control Agency)
● health surveillance of the population
● and international negotiations on health matters.

5.14 Bodies such as the Health Education Authority in England would continue to be used to help in delivering the health education message relating to healthy eating. In Scotland this responsibility (which will be devolved) would remain with the Health Education Board for Scotland. The delivery of health education in Wales will eventually be a matter for the Welsh Assembly. In Northern Ireland, the Health Promotion Agency for Northern Ireland will be expected to work with the Agency on delivering the health education message.

5.15 The Government intends that there will be very close liaison and active collaboration between Health Departments and the Agency across the whole spectrum of nutrition and related public health issues. This close collaboration, together with the proposed joint secretariat for COMA, will ensure that a consistent health message is provided to the public. The Agency may also be able to make useful links with Health Departments' oral health work in its public education activities.

Chapter 6: The Structure of the Agency and its Accountability

6.1 Professor James recommended that the Agency should be established as a non-departmental public body (NDPB) with executive powers. He suggested that its structure should be loosely based on the Health and Safety Commission/Health and Safety Executive (HSC/HSE) model, but noted that this would need to be adapted to suit the rather different circumstances of the food safety area. He recommended that the Commission of the Agency should have strengthened operational autonomy, as compared with HSC; that it should not have to seek Ministers' approval of its work plan and that it would have the right to publish its advice, for which it would be accountable. He envisaged that the Commission would consist of around ten members appointed after consultation with consumer and public interest groups, representatives of the food industry, the Leader of the Opposition and the Chair of the relevant Parliamentary Select Committee. Although the Commission should include people with a background in industry, public and consumer interests should be in the majority. The Commission should also include representatives of Scotland, Wales and Northern Ireland.

6.2 Professor James proposed that the Agency should report to Parliament through Health Ministers, with the Secretary of State for Health taking the lead. In order to recognise the substantial and legitimate interest of other Ministers, including the Minister of Agriculture, Fisheries and Food, in the policy area, he suggested that a Ministerial Council, including the Secretaries of State for Scotland, Wales and Northern Ireland, the Agriculture Minister and other interested Ministers, and chaired by the Secretary of State for Health, should be established to provide an appropriate reporting mechanism.

6.3 Responses to the consultation exercise were generally broadly in favour of basing the Agency on the HSC/HSE model. Many responses stressed the need to adapt the model to the complex area of food safety and standards.

6.4 The composition of the Commission attracted particular interest, with clear support from most respondents (other than industry interests) for the proposal that public and consumer interests should be in the majority. Respondents from particular sectors were anxious to see their own interests well represented on the Commission. However, a number of respondents stressed that it was important to appoint Commissioners on the basis of their skills and experience rather than as representatives of particular groups. Some respondents expressed concern that the arrangements for a Ministerial Council might be over-complex or lead to a lack of clarity over management arrangements.

Form and composition of the Agency

6.5 The Government agrees that the Agency should be a public body with advisory and executive powers and that its structure should be based on the HSC/HSE model, subject to two modifications set out below which reflect the different circumstances of the new Agency. The Government proposes that it will be known as the Food Standards Agency.

The composition and role of the Agency's Commission

6.6 Members of the Health and Safety Commission are appointed by the Secretary of State after consultation with representatives of employees, employers, local authorities and other relevant bodies. While this approach works well in the Health and Safety at Work area, the Government does not believe that it is appropriate for the Food Standards Agency. The range of interests affected by the Agency is extremely wide, and it would not be feasible for the membership of the Commission to cover all the relevant fields. The Government intends therefore that the Commission should consist of a body of individuals who have a proven track record in relevant fields who together provide a reasonable balance of relevant skills and experience, and a majority of whom come from a wider public interest background without any specific affiliation. The Commissioners will take expert advice from the well-established network of independent Advisory Committees (described in Annex 2, Appendix 2) and will consult widely in order to ensure that their decisions are based on the best possible scientific advice. Four new Advisory Committees are proposed, to provide advice on the implications for Scotland, Wales and Northern Ireland of the Agency's activities and to advise the Agency and Agriculture Ministers on all matters affecting the safety, quality and efficacy of animal feedingstuffs.

6.7 The Government intends that the Commission should comprise a Chairperson and no more than twelve members. They would be appointed by UK Health Ministers, acting jointly with the Secretary of State for Health taking the lead, and after consultation with Agriculture Ministers. Appointments would be made in accordance with the guidance issued by the Commissioner for Public Appointments (the Nolan principles and Peach rules). The Commission would work collectively to further the aims and objectives of the Agency, which in turn will reflect the Guiding Principles set out in Chapter 2. The Commission would reach its decisions collectively, but individual Commissioners would be expected to take a special interest in particular areas of the Agency's work as well as maintaining a broad overview. In particular, individual Commissioners would have special responsibility for Scottish, Welsh and Northern Ireland interests, in addition to providing skills or experience in an area which is relevant to the Agency's national role (see Chapter 7).

The legal structure of the Commission and Executive

6.8 The Health and Safety Commission and Health and Safety Executive are two separate legal entities. Only the HSC can provide advice to Ministers. However, the HSC is precluded by statute from intervening in specific enforcement decisions, though it sets the broad policy and resource framework for the enforcement activities of the Executive. This is because of the representative nature of the Commission, the need to avoid it being involved in enforcement decisions which could occasionally suggest a possible conflict of interest, and to ensure that it focuses on a strategic, policy role.

6.9 The Government does not consider that a formal separation between the Commission and the Executive is appropriate in the circumstances of the Food Standards Agency. The Commission is likely to become directly involved in significant operational matters dealt with by the Agency, and it will be important for the Commission itself to be seen to be accountable for the actions taken by the Agency on this sort of issue.

6.10 In order to ensure that the Commission is clearly responsible for the operations of the Agency the Government intends to establish it as a single legal entity, and to endow the Commission with all of the Agency's policy and executive powers. It would be for the Commission, acting collectively, to determine the extent to which it delegated responsibility for day to day operational matters to the Chief Executive and his/her staff. This arrangement would not give rise to the conflicts of interest which might occur with a model based on the HSC/HSE, because the Agency's Commissioners will not have a formal representative role which could be seen as colouring their approach to the business of the Agency. The Agency's internal structure will need to reflect the nature of its functions, including clear lines of responsibility for enforcement (including licensing) decisions, and clear separation between operational and audit roles. Overall these arrangements will ensure that the staff of the Agency are accountable to the Commission for the discharge of all their functions.

6.11   In particular the Meat Hygiene Service will continue to operate as a separate entity, managed on Next Steps principles, with its own Chief Executive who will report to the Commission. The MHS will continue to be audited by the Veterinary Public Health Unit within the Agency.

Accountability mechanisms

Relationship with Ministers

6.12   The Government agrees that the Agency should report to Health Ministers, with the Secretary of State for Health taking the lead. The Agency's role, its relationship with its sponsor Department and the financial arrangements which apply to it will be clearly set out in a Management Statement and Financial Memorandum which will be publicly available. The Agency will be required to produce an Annual Report, Corporate Plan and Business Plan and will be subject to an annual accountability review and a more fundamental quinquennial review. The Agency will be expected to consult with Health Departments over the production of its Annual Report and Business Plans, and to consider any comments which they wished to make on the draft Annual Report, but would not be bound to make any changes in response to such comments. In accordance with the normal arrangements for ensuring financial accountability, the Corporate and Business Plans would be subject to joint agreement by Health Ministers, who would consult other Ministers as appropriate. In addition the Agency would be required to meet specified performance targets relating to efficiency and quality.

6.13   It is important to ensure that the Agency's advice is taken fully into account in the formulation of policy across the complete range of food-related issues. To facilitate this, staff of the Agency will participate fully in the normal Whitehall-wide machinery for co-ordinating policy. This will ensure that the Agency has a significant input in policy issues in which it has an interest. It will also provide a mechanism whereby the Agency, if it wishes, can seek assistance in ensuring that its work is consistent with its guiding principles (for example that it complies with the United Kingdom's obligations under international law).

6.14   The Ministerial Group on Food Safety, chaired by the Chancellor of the Duchy of Lancaster, which has overseen the preparations for the Agency, has provided an effective means of ensuring that Departments work together in pursuance of a coherent policy. The Government does not consider it necessary to have a separate statutory mechanism for the co-ordination of policy issues. Similar arrangements to the existing Ministerial Committees will provide the forum for the discussion of any issues which need to be considered collectively by Ministers. These arrangements will be adapted as necessary to reflect the post-devolution co-operation arrangements foreshadowed in the Devolution White Papers.

6.15   The Agency will, as Professor James recommended, be free to make public its advice to Ministers who would then have to explain in public their reasons for any decision not to accept that advice. This freedom will provide a powerful guarantee of the Agency's independence and will enable it to exercise considerable influence. The Government attaches great importance to the Agency's freedom to offer whatever advice it thinks necessary in the public interest, without interference from political or business interests.

6.16   However, as indicated in Chapter 2 above, the Government sees a need to introduce a mechanism to prevent the Agency from acting, or proposing to act, in a way which was inconsistent with its Guiding Principles and which would therefore not be in the wider public interest. The Government proposes that Health Ministers should be given powers of direction over the Agency which could be exercised only if the Agency appears to act outside the terms of its specific legal framework.

Parliamentary Accountability

6.17 The Agency's Annual Report would be laid before Parliament, and before the Scottish Parliament, the Welsh Assembly and any devolved assembly in Northern Ireland. The Agency will advise Health Ministers to enable them to respond to Parliamentary Questions about the Agency's work, as and when it is appropriate for them to reply substantively. Health Ministers will present legislation proposed by the Agency to Parliament. The Chairperson of the Commission might be invited to give evidence to Parliamentary Select Committees. The Chief Executive would be the Agency's Accounting Officer. It would be for Parliament itself to consider Professor James's suggestion that a Select Committee on Food should be established to monitor the Agency's activities. The Scottish Parliament and the Welsh Assembly will have powers to hold the Agency to account in the same way as the Westminster Parliament, as would any devolved assembly in Northern Ireland.

Location of the Agency

6.18 Professor James recommended that the headquarters of the Agency should be located in London, in the expectation that it will need to maintain close contact with Ministers and officials around Whitehall. He identified a risk of the Agency becoming marginalised if its headquarters were outside London.

6.19 The Government agrees that the Agency will need to maintain close contact with Whitehall and intends therefore to locate its headquarters in London. The Executives in Scotland, Wales and Northern Ireland will be located in these countries, and the Agency will also have, through the Meat Hygiene Service, a presence in York and a number of regional offices in England, Scotland and Wales.

The Agency's Staff

6.20 Professor James emphasised that the Agency's staff should be responsible to the Commission, not to Ministers; that while staff could be transferred from Government Departments to the Agency it would be important to effect a culture change by including an appropriate mix of existing expertise and new appointments; and that the Chief Executive should be appointed by the Commission and should be a Crown Office Holder not in a civil service career path.

6.21 The Government agrees that the staff of the Agency should be accountable to the Commission rather than to Ministers. It believes that the changes in policy which have been introduced since the Government took office in May 1997, some of which are described in Chapter 9, are already contributing to the change in culture which Professor James calls for. It agrees however that it will be important for the Agency to continue the process of developing a fully open and transparent culture in which protection of public health is, and is seen as, the essential aim. The Agency will therefore need to supplement the expertise which transfers from Departments by making some new appointments.

6.22 The Government intends that the staff of the Agency should be civil servants. The nature of much of the Agency's work — in particular provision of advice to Ministers, preparation of legislation and representation of the UK in EC and international negotiations — is identical to that of many Government Departments and requires the policy and administrative skills in which civil servants are trained. It will be important for some interchange of staff to take place with Departments, for example of public health doctors and veterinarians, in order to ensure that the Agency's culture and policies percolate into related parts of Government. Such interchange will be easier to achieve if the Agency is staffed by civil servants.

6.23 The Government considers that the Commission will be the key element in securing the Agency's culture of openness and independence. However, the Chief Executive will also have a major part to play. He/she will be appointed on a fixed-term contract by open competition and like the other staff of the Agency will be accountable to the Commission, not to Ministers.

6.24   The Government has considered Professor James's recommendation that the Chief Executive should be a Crown Office Holder. However, it believes that Crown Office Holder status could confuse the Chief Executive's line of accountability to the Commission, which will be responsible for all the activities of the Agency and will determine the extent to which responsibility will be delegated to the Chief Executive. It is the Commission, not the Chief Executive, which will be accountable to Parliament for the Agency's activities, as described in paragraph 6.17. The Government does not therefore intend to designate the Chief Executive as a Crown Office Holder.

Chapter 7 :
The Agency in Scotland, Wales and Northern Ireland

7.1 Professor James identified the need for the Agency's structure to reflect the constitutional arrangements in the different parts of the United Kingdom and to allow any future elected bodies in Scotland, Wales or Northern Ireland to make their own assessment of policy and legislation which has been developed on a UK basis or in Europe and to initiate work on any particular Scottish, Welsh or Northern Irish issues which may arise. However, he also stressed the importance of consistency of standards, enforcement, policy and advice throughout the United Kingdom, and proposed that Ministers in Westminster and Ministers from any devolved Parliament or Assembly should not be able to legislate in areas within the Agency's remit without consulting the Agency's Commission. He recommended that there should be separate Commissions in Scotland, Wales and Northern Ireland and that the UK Commission should include representatives from Scotland, Wales and Northern Ireland who would also be members of the appropriate Commission. Each of the Commissions would have its own small executive staff who would advise them.

7.2 Responses to the consultation reflected a variety of views on the proposal for separate territorial structures. Broadly speaking, respondents representing interests in Scotland, Wales and Northern Ireland supported the concept of separate structures, noting that different legal systems and other arrangements made these necessary. Respondents representing UK food industry interests or purely English interests (such as English local authorities) generally preferred a single UK body which would allow for proper co-ordination of work, avoid the risk of inconsistency and provide for greater efficiency. Some responses suggested that an additional body for England, to parallel those proposed for Scotland, Wales and Northern Ireland, might be appropriate. There was general recognition of the need for consistency and a widespread acceptance that this could be best achieved by the UK Agency taking a central strategic and co-ordinating role.

7.3 In the context of devolution, it has been agreed that food standards will be devolved to the future Scottish Parliament, and that the Welsh Assembly will inherit powers on food standards from the Secretary of State for Wales, including the power to make secondary legislation. In Northern Ireland, food standards issues, including the development of primary and secondary legislation and codes of practice, are already the responsibility of the Northern Ireland administration.

7.4 Modern methods of food distribution are such that foodstuffs produced in one part of the United Kingdom are frequently sold in another. Consistency in policy and enforcement across the United Kingdom is therefore essential for consumers and for the food industry. The network of Advisory Committees needs to draw upon the full range of expertise available throughout the UK (and sometimes outside it). If food safety and standards policies are to be consistent a single body — the UK Agency — needs to receive the scientific advice and formulate proposals for legislation or other action. The consultation exercise suggests that this is generally accepted to be necessary.

7.5 The Government proposes therefore that the Agency should be established as a UK body, with full participation by Ministers in Scotland, Wales and Northern Ireland and their successors from devolved Parliaments or Assemblies in its accountability mechanisms (as described in Chapter 6) and with appropriate arrangements to reflect the particular needs and interests of those countries. In the case of Scotland, while devolution will mean that the Scottish Parliament will have the power to decide through primary legislation on different arrangements, the Government believes that its proposals will be recognised as effectively combining the advantages of a single UK Agency in this sensitive area with the benefits of full involvement by the devolved Parliament and administration.

7.6 The UK Agency would be responsible for advising the Government on the UK policy framework on food standards and safety matters.

7.7 The Government proposes that:

- the UK Commission should include members who have special responsibility for Scottish, Welsh and Northern Irish interests, in addition to providing skills or experience in areas which are relevant to the Agency's national role
- Advisory Committees should be set up in Scotland, Wales and Northern Ireland. These Committees would provide a focus for Scottish, Welsh and Northern Irish interests in food standards and would advise the UK Commission. They would be set up on a statutory basis with a defined remit which would reflect the responsibilities of the UK Agency. Their membership would reflect the range of interests on food safety issues in Scotland, Wales and Northern Ireland. The chairperson of each Committee would be a member of the UK Commission and the Committees' advice would normally be channelled to the UK Commission through the Commissioners with specific responsibility for their interests
- the Advisory Committees would be invited to express a view on all proposals for legislative change, and these views would be reported to Ministers in Scotland, Wales and Northern Ireland when the UK Agency put forward proposals for any such changes. These Ministers, and their successors from any devolved Parliament or Assembly, could also seek advice on any issues relevant to food standards and safety from these Committees. The Committees could also be asked to offer advice on specific Scottish,

Welsh or Northern Irish issues which arise in any of the other Advisory Committees
- there would be Food Standards Agency Executives in Scotland, Wales and Northern Ireland which would each be part of the UK FSA Executive. They would each be headed by FSA Directors who would report to the Chief Executive of the UK Agency. The Executives would take over responsibility for the existing food safety and standards functions carried out by the Scottish, Welsh and Northern Ireland Offices; monitor food law enforcement activities and liaise with local authorities and other enforcement bodies; provide the secretariat for their Advisory Committees; and advise Ministers or their successors from any devolved Parliament or Assembly. The work of the FSA Executives in each country would reflect that country's distinctive legislative and administrative arrangements
- in Northern Ireland the FSA Executive would take over NI Departments' current responsibilities for advising the Secretary of State for Northern Ireland on the development of legislation and Codes of Practice for Northern Ireland, based on the preparatory work done by the UK Headquarters. Similar arrangements would apply after Devolution in Scotland and Wales
- in advising Ministers or their successors on the implications for Scotland, Wales or Northern Ireland of the Agency's proposals for legislation, the Executives would take full account of the advice of the appropriate Advisory Committee
- these Executives would operate within the overarching policy framework established by the UK Agency
- the different food inspection and enforcement systems in the different parts of the United Kingdom would continue.

7.8 Health Ministers or their successors under Devolution after consultation with Agriculture Ministers, would statutorily:

- appoint the chairman of the UK Commission
- appoint other Commission members, including those with special responsibility for Scottish, Welsh or Northern Irish interests. The Government envisages that there would be two Commissioners with specific responsibility for Scottish interests and at least one each with specific responsibility for Welsh and Northern Irish interests
- appoint the first Chief Executive of the UK Agency, and the first Directors of the Executives in Scotland, Wales and Northern Ireland
- exercise any other statutory functions associated with the Food Standards Agency, including Orders under food safety and standards legislation and terms of reference of the various Food Standards Agency bodies, including the UK Commission, the Scottish, Welsh and Northern Irish Advisory Committees and the scientific Advisory Committees.

7.9 The Secretaries of State for Scotland, Wales and Northern Ireland, or successors under Devolution, would appoint respectively the representatives on the Scottish, Welsh and Northern Ireland FSA Committees who are not members of the UK Commission.

7.10 Following Devolution, any changes to the statutory basis of the Agency would require the agreement of the Scottish Parliament and consultation with the Welsh Assembly and any devolved assembly in Northern Ireland. The Scottish Parliament will have the power to carry through primary and secondary legislation in devolved areas, including food standards legislation, and the Welsh Assembly will have the power to carry through secondary legislation.

Separate and parallel orders will therefore normally be needed in the Scottish Parliament and the Welsh Assembly. Food standards legislation will continue to be made separately in Northern Ireland.

7.11 In summary, the Government's proposals are designed to ensure that food standards policy continues to be developed and implemented coherently and consistently across the United Kingdom while providing for Scotland, Wales and Northern Ireland each to have:

- identifiable participation in the UK Commission
- its own Food Standards Advisory Committee which would advise the Agency and others, including Ministers, on request on food safety and standards issues within its remit
- FSA Executives which are part of the UK Executive, responsible for operational issues working within the legislative and policy framework established by the UK Agency
- as appropriate to local circumstances, its own distinctive systems for food inspection and enforcement.

7.12 The Government believes that these arrangements provide suitably robust and effective mechanisms to enable the particular interests of Scotland, Wales and Northern Ireland to be taken fully into account in the activities of the UK Agency, and to enable decisions on operational issues in these countries to be taken there, rather than in London.

Chapter 8:
Financing the Agency

The financial framework

8.1 Professor James recommended that funding for the Agency should come from the Department of Health budget by a mechanism which is open to public scrutiny. He stressed that the funding mechanism should ensure the effectiveness of the Agency and suggested that its funding requirement might be stated publicly in the Corporate Plan.

8.2 The Government agrees that the Department of Health should be lead sponsor department and therefore that the Secretary of State for Health should be responsible, through the normal parliamentary supply procedures, for providing grant-in-aid to the Agency. Resources associated with existing activities currently carried out by MAFF will need to be transferred to DH. In addition, the Agency will be financed by other sources, for example charges to the food industry.

8.3 The precise mechanisms for funding the Agency in Scotland, Wales and Northern Ireland are still under consideration. Arrangements will be required to provide financial resources for the functions which will transfer from the Scottish, Welsh and Northern Ireland Offices to the Agency. Procedures will also be required to review future levels of activity and associated funding levels in Scotland, Wales and Northern Ireland. These will need to take into account the interest of the proposed Scottish Parliament and Welsh Assembly.

8.4 The Government agrees that the Agency's Corporate Plan should be published, in addition to its Annual Report and Accounts, so that information about the Agency's finances and strategies is available to Parliament and other interested parties. However, this process should not be allowed to hinder Parliament's role of deciding how resources should be allocated between competing demands across all areas of policy.

The costs of the Agency

8.5 Although final decisions on the exact functions and responsibilities of the Agency will not be taken until after consultation on this White Paper has ended, the core work of the Agency will include the activities of those parts of MAFF and DH which go to make up the Joint Food Safety and Standards Group, together with the Meat Hygiene Service. The Agency will also take on some new activities and develop other areas of work and will therefore require additional resources over time.

8.6 As well as the activities currently carried out by civil servants in Departments, the Agency is likely to take over budgetary responsibility for commissioning a range of activities performed outside its own organisation. The largest items here will be research and surveillance programmes. The principle to be followed will be that where the Agency takes over this sort of responsibility from Departments, the relevant budgetary resources will also be transferred.

8.7 The Agency will have one-off start-up costs. Their level will depend on decisions to be taken in the light of this White Paper. The creation of the Agency will also inevitably lead to new on-going costs. While some of the existing administrative costs (eg office support) may be partially offset by savings within Departments, others — such as the costs associated with the Commission — will not.

8.8 As a result of the proposals outlined elsewhere in this White Paper, the Agency will be expected to take on a number of new activities and the Agency itself will no doubt identify other areas where it wishes to undertake new or expanded activities. For example, over time, costs will arise from:

- the Agency's public information and education roles
- its role in ensuring that public health issues are taken into account by other Government Departments and Agencies with responsibilities relevant to food safety

- its responsibilities for setting standards for enforcement and auditing the work done by local authorities
- any new surveillance activity and/or follow up work which it decides to initiate.

The precise costs involved will depend on the decisions taken following consultation on this White Paper and on how the Agency decides to carry out its responsibilities.

8.9   Taking all of these factors into account and subject to further decisions still to be taken, the Agency's total projected annual expenditure is estimated to be in excess of £100 million. Of this, about £35 million is currently recovered through charges to industry, including those made by the MHS. The remaining costs of the existing activities fall to the Agriculture and Health Departments' budgets.

Local authorities' costs

8.10   In addition, significant resources are committed to food safety and standards work through local government funding. This is not separately recorded, because Environmental Health Departments and Trading Standards Departments have other responsibilities as well as those relating to food. However, current local authority expenditure on food safety and standards enforcement is estimated at £120 million to £150 million per annum.

8.11   There was a degree of support in the responses to the consultation exercise for Professor James's proposals on ring-fencing funding for food safety and standards work at local authority level. While the Government recognises the arguments in this direction, it takes a view on this subject against the background of priorities for local government spending as a whole and does not think it appropriate to ring-fence local authority expenditure on enforcement and surveillance.

8.12   However, the Government recognises that the Agency's work to raise standards may lead to a

need for greater expenditure at local level. The position will, of course, vary across the UK depending on local circumstances. In Northern Ireland, there is at present some ring-fencing of funding for food safety work.

Meeting the costs

8.13   The creation of the Agency, with the consequence that additional costs will arise, means that it is necessary to look again at the sources of funding for regulatory and enforcement activity in the area of food standards and safety.

8.14   The food industry's production and distribution processes are designed to ensure that food meets the quality and safety standards required by legislation and their customers. The production costs associated with meeting these standards already fall to industry, as do some of the costs associated with running the regulatory regime, such as the cost of meat hygiene inspections and, in England and Wales, milk hygiene inspections. The EU is moving towards charging for other types of hygiene inspection, for example fisheries products, but the great majority of the central and local government costs are currently borne out of the public purse.

8.15   Against the background of a need for increased spending on the regulatory and enforcement activities carried out at national and local level, the Government believes that the food industry should bear the bulk of the costs of improving food safety and standards. The food industry as a whole will benefit from the improved public confidence in food safety and standards that the Agency is likely to bring. The Government is therefore considering possible mechanisms for passing on a greater part of the costs of food safety work directly to the food industry, recognising that over time the bulk of these costs are likely to be passed on to the consumer.

8.16   A substantial proportion of the current cost of food safety work, particularly in the local authority sector, is accounted for by enforcement

inspections and licensing or approval schemes under the Food Safety Act 1990 and the Regulations and Codes of Practice made under that Act. Some of this work is subject to charging, for example for meat inspection, but in many areas the taxpayer currently meets the cost.

8.17 The Government therefore considers that the most appropriate mechanism for shifting the burden of cost away from the taxpayer towards the industry would be to introduce a comprehensive system of registration or licensing with fees. Such a scheme would both extend and consolidate the existing registration, approval and licensing arrangements, provide additional resources to meet the new costs associated with the Agency, and enable local authorities to take action to improve food safety standards. As the main responsibility for enforcement inspections outside the fresh meat sector rests with local authorities, they would be the natural point for registering or licensing businesses and collecting fees. The Government intends to seek the assistance of local authority representatives, as well as representatives of the food industry (including small businesses) and other interested parties in developing its proposals for a scheme.

8.18 The Government firmly intends to shift the burden of cost away from the taxpayer in this way. However, a number of questions will require detailed discussion and consultation before the Government finalises its proposals. These include:

- the scope of the scheme
- the extent to which the issue of a licence should be subject to conditions
- the frequency with which licences might be subject to renewal
- alternatively, the case for a simple fee-based registration scheme
- whether the licence or registration fee should relate to the business premises or to a named individual or company
- the relationship between this scheme and other licensing and approval requirements

in UK and EU legislation so as to build on existing arrangements and avoid unnecessary bureaucracy
- the basis on which charges would be calculated, including the need to take into account the size of the business
- the mechanism for transferring part of the income from the charges to the Agency, while ensuring that sufficient resources are retained by local authorities to cover any additional costs they incurred in operating the scheme.

8.19 The Government expects that the income from the scheme would be used to offset the costs associated with the Agency, including any new surveillance, enforcement or other activity which the Agency initiates to improve food safety standards across the country. Because of the uncertainties discussed in paragraph 8.5 to 8.8 above, it is not possible at this stage to give precise estimates of the amount which would need to be raised. However the potential impact on individual businesses can be tentatively illustrated by the following example. There are around 600,000 food premises in the UK (ranging from manufacturing plants to caterers and retail shops) registered with local authorities. If the scheme were to apply to all of these premises, a flat rate fee of £100 per premises per annum would raise around £60 million. Even after the administrative costs of operating the scheme were taken into account, this would offset a substantial amount of new activity by the Agency.

8.20 The Government intends to formulate detailed proposals in the light of its discussions with all interested parties on these questions, and will publish them for further consultation. While a licensing or registration scheme might be the most appropriate mechanism for shifting the burden of the cost of food safety work away from the taxpayer, the Government would be interested to hear alternative practical suggestions of ways of passing on part of the costs of food safety work to the food industry.

Chapter 9 :
The Way Ahead

9.1   Following the very useful first round of consultation on the James Report, this White Paper forms the second phase of consultation on the proposal to set up a Food Standards Agency. A Bill to establish the Agency, to endow it with the legal powers required for it to fulfil its responsibilities, and to make the changes necessary to the current allocation of responsibilities between Health and Agriculture Ministers, will be drafted in the light of responses to this White Paper and will be published as the third stage of consultation.

9.2   The Bill will be brought before Parliament as soon as Parliamentary time permits; this will not be before the 1998/99 session of Parliament begins. If Parliamentary approval is sought and obtained in the next session of Parliament, the Agency might be launched towards the end of 1999.

9.3   Establishing an Agency with such an important and wide-ranging remit is a complex process. The Government intends to make full use of the time which is required for the preparation and passage of the legislation to continue detailed discussions with representatives of the public, consumer organisations, the enforcement authorities, the scientific community and the food and farming industries. Close co-operation between all those with an interest is essential to achieve a smooth transition and to construct a secure foundation for the new Agency.

9.4   In order to maintain momentum and to achieve a smooth transition, the Government intends to appoint a shadow governing body for the Agency as soon as the Bill has made sufficient progress through Parliament. This shadow governing body would play a major role in the preparations for launching the Agency itself.

9.5   In the meantime the Government has already taken, and will continue to take, steps to strengthen the handling of food issues and to deliver real improvements in the information that is given to the public, the advice that Ministers receive and the decisions that are taken. In particular:

- Ministers in MAFF and DH are determined that the two Departments should work together cohesively and in a mutually supportive way. The Minister for Food Safety, Jeff Rooker, and the Minister for Public Health, Tessa Jowell are therefore working as a team, both in driving forward preparations for the Agency and in overseeing the day-to-day food safety work of their Departments, with the full support of the Minister of Agriculture, Fisheries and Food, Jack Cunningham, and the Secretary of State for Health, Frank Dobson. They are liaising closely with their counterparts in Scotland, Wales and Northern Ireland to ensure a consistent approach across the UK

- On 1 September 1997, a new MAFF and Department of Health Joint Food Safety and Standards Group was set up. This Group has brought together into a cohesive whole those parts of the two Departments that are likely to form the operational core of the new Agency. In Scotland food safety activities are currently brigaded in a single group within the Scottish Office, under the responsibility of the Scottish Health Minister. In Wales, food safety falls within the responsibility of the Welsh Health Minister. In Northern Ireland the Minister with responsibility for health takes the lead on food safety

- The Chief Medical Officer for England has taken on a new high-level co-ordinating role on food and health issues, to ensure that information about matters affecting human health is presented clearly and comprehensively to the public. In this role he will be working closely with the Chief Medical Officers in the other UK Health Departments

- A new joint MAFF/DH Risk Communication Unit is being created. The Chief Medical Officer has particular responsibility for this unit, and an external adviser is being appointed

- The role of the independent Advisory Committees which advise Government on food safety related matters is being further developed and strengthened. Lay membership of these committees is being increased, with lay appointments being made to the Spongiform Encephalopathy Advisory Committee, the Advisory Committee on Pesticides and the Veterinary Products Committee

- Government has accepted all the recommendations of the Pennington Report on the E.coli outbreak in central Scotland. A number of these have already been implemented, including a substantial funding package for enhanced enforcement in retail premises handling raw and cooked meat

- the emphasis on greater openness is being carried through in policy decisions such as the publication of brand names in reports on food surveillance and, from January 1998, Hygiene Assessment System scores for abattoirs and cutting plants.

9.6 The fundamental principles that will govern the Agency are, in effect, already being applied to all the Government's actions and decisions on food safety and standard issues.

Annex 1 : The James Report

1. In March this year, the Prime Minister, while Leader of the Opposition, invited Professor Philip James of the Rowett Research Institute in Aberdeen to make recommendations on the structure and functions of a Food Standards Agency. His report was formally presented to the Prime Minister on 8 May and immediately published for consultation. The Prime Minister gave his firm support to the general thrust of Professor James's proposals and commented:

"The public has the right to expect the very highest standards of food safety. Confidence in the safety of the food we eat has been severely undermined in recent years, and I am determined to rebuild that trust.

"I thank Professor James for his detailed and considered report. It provides an excellent foundation upon which the Government can build. It confirms my belief that we will benefit from a powerful Food Standards Agency. We need to create a structure that is open and transparent, and which acts — and is seen to act — in the interests of consumers."

2. This annex summarises the key recommendations in Professor James's report and the main features of the public response to the consultation.

Professor James's key recommendations

- The Agency should advise Ministers on all matters relating to food safety, food standards, and nutrition and public health; its remit should encompass the complete food chain
- It should be a statutory Non-Departmental Public Body with executive powers, reporting to Parliament through Health Ministers, with the Secretary of State for Health taking the lead
- The Agency should be governed by a Commission which includes representatives from Scotland, Wales and Northern

Ireland and in which consumer and public interest nominees are in the majority

- Arrangements should be put in place in Scotland, Wales and Northern Ireland to assess policy and legislation emerging from the UK Agency and the EC from a territorial perspective and to initiate work on particular territorial issues. The Agency's role should include developing policy, proposing and drafting legislation, and public education and information on matters within its remit
- The Agency should be responsible for co-ordinating, monitoring and auditing local food law enforcement activities
- The Agency should co-ordinate all the research in the food safety, nutrition and consumer protection area
- Funding for the Agency should come through the Department of Health budget by a mechanism which is open to public scrutiny.

Public response to the report

3. The public consultation exercise confirmed the widespread interest in, and broad support for, Professor James's recommendations. Well over 600 replies were received, from a very wide range of interests including consumers, public health medicine, local government, veterinary services, scientific research, all sectors of the food production and distribution industries and a significant number of private individuals. Appendix 1 to this Annex lists the respondents to the consultation exercise.

4. Respondents were almost unanimous in agreeing that substantial reform of the existing arrangements was desirable. While there was wide support for Professor James's analysis of the current problems, many respondents stressed that the problems arose from a loss of confidence in the Government machinery for handling food safety issues, rather than a loss of confidence in British food.

5. Respondents firmly supported Professor James's view that there should be a clearer separation in Government between responsibility for promoting food safety and responsibility for promoting the interests of the food and related industries. There was broad agreement that a statutory Non-Departmental Public Body, operating on an open and transparent basis, could provide an effective vehicle for improving food safety and standards and thus restoring confidence.

6. Many respondents stressed that the new Agency must remain accountable to Parliament through Ministers. A substantial majority agreed that Health Ministers should take the lead, but a minority recommended that the Agency should report through another Minister, such as a Minister for Food, a Consumer Affairs Minister or a Cabinet Office Minister.

7. There was general agreement that food safety issues (including microbiological, chemical and radiological safety, genetically modified foods and novel foods and processes) should be at the core of the Agency's responsibilities. There was overall agreement with the principle that the Agency should promote food safety throughout the entire food chain. There was considerable debate on whether the Agency's remit should extend beyond food safety to include food standards issues such as compositional and labelling requirements, and nutrition and diet questions. Some respondents argued that the Agency's remit should include all matters related to food production and distribution which are of interest to consumers (including, for example standards of agricultural practice such as animal welfare and the environmental impact of food production). Other respondents felt that the Agency should concentrate exclusively on matters of microbiological and chemical food safety. They felt that a wider remit would dilute the Agency's focus and therefore reduce its effectiveness.

8. Respondents agreed that the Agency should be responsible for providing advice to Ministers and for education and information to the public on food safety matters. However, views differed on whether the Agency should be given wider executive functions, for example in drafting legislation and negotiating in the EU and other international fora.

RESPONDENTS TO CONSULTATION ON THE JAMES REPORT

Organisation	Name
Aberdeen City Council	Michie N.
Aberdeenshire Council	McDonald I.
Academic Unit of Paediatric Oncology	Eden O.
Advertising Association	Bas J.
Advisory Body for Social Services Catering	Denton R.
Agricultural Engineers Association	Vowles J.
Agricultural Engineers Association	Saunders R.
Allerdale Borough Council	Daley P.
Altnagelvin Hospitals Health and Social Services Trust	McColgan E.
Analytical Services (South Wales)	Lenartowicz P.
Anaphylaxis Campaign	Reading D.
Animal Health Distributors Association UK	Dawson R.
Animal Medicines Training Regulatory Authority	Dawson R.
Argyle & Bute Council	Taylor S.
Argyle and Clyde Health Board	Vinson M.
Aries Services	Taylor J.
Armagh District Council	Briggs W.
Association of Greater Manchester Authorities	Fletcher D.
Association of Ind. Crop Consultants	Smiley F.
Association of Local Authorities Northern Ireland	McKay R.
Association of Port Health Authorities	Rotheram P.
Association of Public Analysts	Harrison N.
Association of Public Analysts Scotland	Grant J.
Association of State Veterinary Officers	McVicar C.
Association of Veterinary Surgeons Practising in Northern Ireland	Laughlin K.
Association for Public Health	Reid D.
Association of Community Health Council	Harris T.
Association of Medical Microbiologists	Tompkins D.
Association of Public Analysts of Scotland	Grant J.
Aston University	Jepson M.
Automatic Vending Association of Britain	Gledhill J.
Aylesbury Vale District Council	Brown S.
Ayrshire and Arran Health Board	Smellie M.
BACFID	Kendrick C.
Banbridge District Council	Forbes K.
Barking and Havering Health Authority	Kangesu E.
Bedfordshire County Council	Davies C.
Belfast City Council	Francey W.
Belfast City Hospital	Wilson T.
Belfast Health and Social Services Trust	Black R.
Bexley Council	Osborne J.

Organisation	Name
BIBRA/British Toxicological Society	Jaggers S.
Biotechnology and Biological Sciences Research Council	Baker R.
Biscuit, Cake, Chocolate and Confectionery Alliance	Newman T.
Blackburn with Darwen Borough Council	Nathan T.
Bolton Metro Environmental Health Services	Clegg J.
Bournemouth Borough Council	Kitchin J.
Bournemouth University	Jones P.
Bradford City Metropolitan District Council	Armstrong R.
Brentwood Borough Council	Bennett S.
Brewers and Licensed Retailers Association	Rawlings M
BRF International	Righelato R.
British Agrochemicals Association	Leitch D.
British Association of Feed Supplement and Additive Manufacturers	Beaumont W.
British Crop Protection Council	Finney J.
British Dental Association	Sole E.
British Dietetic Association	Cowbrough K.
British Egg Industry Council	Ring M.
British Frozen Food Federation	Farley I.
British Goat Society	Goodwin R.
British Heart Foundation	Pentecost B.
British Heart Foundation Health Promotion Group	Rayner M.
British Hospitality Association	Logie J.
British Meat Manufacturers Association	Sunley E.
British Medical Association	Hartley C.
British Medical Association	Lowe M.
British Medical Association Scottish Office	Cook H.
British Nutrition Foundation	Wharton B.
British Pest Control Association	Strand R.
British Pig Association	Welsh G.
British Ports Association	Whitehead D.
British Retail Consortium	Nunn J.
British Society for Allergy Environmental and Nutritional Medicine	Anthony H.
British Veterinary Association	Linklater K.
Bro Taf Health Authority	Evans M.
Bromley Health Authority	Bhan A.
BSI Quality Assurance	Wright N.
Buckinghamshire Health Authority	Haworth E
Bury Metropolitan Council	Freer W.
Caerphilly County Borough Council	Mitchard R.
Calderdale and Kirklees Health Authority	Barnes G.
Calderdale Council	Collinge R.
Cambridge University	McConnell I.
Camden & Islington Health Authority	Bahl M.
Campden and Chorleywood Food Research Association	Stringer M.

Organisation	Name
Cannington College	Fray M.
Cardiff Business Partnership	Holland D.
Cardiff County Council	Evans V.
Central Scientific Laboratories	Barnett M.
Central Veterinary Laboratory	Bradley R.
Centre for Applied Microbiology and Research	Gilmour R.
Chartered Institute of Environmental Health	Statham D.
Chartered Institute of Environmental Health	Catanzaro T.
Chartered Institute of Environmental Health	Cooke M.
Chelmsford Borough Council	Hastings G.
Cheshire and Wirral Communicable Disease Unit	Hunter P.
Cheshire County Council	Manley R.
Chesterfield Borough Council	Richards F.
Chilled Food Association	Goodburn K.
Church of Scotland	Blount G.
City and County of Swansea	Spence J.
Clackmannanshire Council	Cunningham W.
Co-operative Union Ltd	Tilley J.
Co-operative Wholesale Society	Humphries C.
Cold Storage and Distribution Federation	Hutchings J.
Coleraine Borough Council	Montgamery S.
COMA Panel on Child and Maternal Nutrition	Williams A.
Compassion in World Farming	Stevenson P.
Compassion in World Farming	O'Brien T.
Confederation of British Industry	Asherson J.
Consumers Association	Cullum P.
Consumers Committee for Great Britain	Laurence J.
Consumers in Europe Group	Asbury G.
Convention of Scottish Local Authorities	Stone T.
Conwy Borough Council	Squire R.
Cookstown Borough Council	Crawford N.
Copeland Borough Council	White B.
Cornish Guild of Smallholders	Cheeseman J.
Corporation of London	Strachan J.
Corporation of London	Butcher D.
Cotswold District Council	Brennan M.
Council for Responsible Nutrition	Hanssen M.
Country Landowners Association	Bailey A.
Coventry City Council	Green M.
Craigawon Borough Council	Reaney T.
Cranfield University	Baker S.
Croydon Borough Council	Boon D.
Cumbria Trading Standards	Ashcroft P.
Dacorum Borough Council	Ablett M.

Organisation	Name
Dairy Council	Johnston M.
Dairy Industry Federation	Wilson C.
Darlington Borough Council	Pearson B.
Daventry District Council	Arnold M.
Dawnfresh Seafoods	Salvesen A.
Derby City Council	Hopkin A.
Derry City Council	Meehan J.
Doncaster Metropolitan Borough Council	Sprender R.
Dorset County Council	Jaggs B.
Dorset Health Authority	Crook S.
Dorset Health Authority	Dawson A.
Dow Corning	Saunders F.
Down District Council	McCvory W.
Dudley Metropolitan Borough Council	Courtis M.
Dumfries & Galloway Council	Davidson W.
Dumfries & Galloway Health Board	Breen D.
Dundee City Council	Dunn R.
Dundee City Council	Gabriel R.
Dungannon District Council	Burke A.
Dunn Nutrition Centre	Whitehead R.
Dunn Nutrition Centre	Cummings J.
East Ayrshire Council	Stafford W.
East Dunbartonshire Council	Nimmo J.
East Lothian Council	Evans D.
East Midlands Chief Trading Standards Officers Group	Hodge R.
East Northamptonshire Council	Wilcock T.
East Refrewshire Council	House R.
East Riding Health Authority	Peiris V.
Eastbourne Borough Council	Baverstock P.
Easter Weens Enterprises	Curtis J.
Eastern Health and Social Services Board	Kilbane M.
Edinburgh Food Consultancy	Morgan-Jones S.
Enfield and Harringey Health Authority	Sen S.
English National Board for Nursing Midwifery & Health Visiting	Thomas M.
English Nature	Cooke A.
Environment Agency (Anglia Region)	Barnden A.
Essex County Council	Wadsley M.
European Food Law Association of the U.K.	Cockbill C.
Exeter City Council	Palfrey R.
Falkirk Council	McClean I.
Fareham Borough Council	Cookson A.
Farm and Food Society	Not Stated
Farm Animal Welfare Network	Druce C.
Farmers Union of Wales	Owen A.

Organisation	Name
Farming and Livestock Concern	Fullerton H.
Federation of Agricultural Co-operatives	Crago T.
Federation of Fresh Meat Wholesalers	Scott P.
Federation of Small Businesses	Robertson R.
Federation of Wholesale Distributors	Toft A.
Fertiliser Manufacturers Association	Salter J.
Fife Council	Barker W.
Finnfeeds International	Thompson A.
Flintshire County Council	Hebden R.
Food & Drink Federation	Mackenzie M.
Food Additives Industry Association	May C.
Food and Agriculture Laboratory Consultative Group	Reed G.
Food Commission	Lobstein T.
Food Control Consultancy	Norman M.
Food for Health Network	Stockley L.
Food Law Group	Holland B.
Food Safety Advisory Centre	Young M.
Food Transport Campaign	Lowery C.
Formanagh District Council	Shaw R.
Fresh Fruit and Vegetable Information Bureau	Parker R.
Fresh Produce Consortium	Henderson D.
Friends of the Earth	Maynard R.
Gateshead Metropolitan Borough Council	Robinson H.
Gedling Borough Council	Nicholson J.
General Consumer Council	Miskell S.
Genetics Forum	Casey S.
Gin and Vodka Association of Great Britain	Wilkinson C.
Glasgow City Council	Kelly B.
Gloucestershire County Council	Galland P.
GMB Union	Hunter D.
Good Taste	Hart D.
Grain & Feed Trade Association	Kirby-Johnson P.
Grampian Health Board	Curnow J.
Grampian Health Board	MacAllan L.
Grampian Health Board	Patterson J.
Greater Glasgow Health Board	Brogan R.
Greater Glasgow NHS Trust	Murphy J.
Green Alliance	Hill J.
Greenpeace	Taylor I.
Guildford Borough Council	Payne N.
Gwent Health Authority	Nehaul L.
Halal Food Authority	Khawaja M.
Hannah Research Institute	Peaker M.
Haringey Council	Munslow N.

Organisation	Name
Harrods	Sherry. M
Harrogate Borough Council	Williamson L.
Hart District Council	Wood N.
Health & Safety Commission	Gates T.
Health Education Board for Scotland	Tannahill A.
Health Food Manufacturers Association	Viner P.
Health Promotion Agency Northern Ireland	Gaffney B.
Health Promotion Service	Linney J.
Health Promotion Wales	Ponton M.
Heinz Ltd	Ritchie M.
Hereford and Worcester County Council	Adams M.
Hertfordshire County Council	Cull N.
Highlands and Islands Enterprise	Robertson I.
Hillsdown Holdings	Greener G.
Holstein Friesian Society of GB and NI	Brigstocke T.
Hotel and Catering International Management Association	Morrison R.
Hull and Goole Port Health Authority	Kaye R.
Ice Cream Federation	Molloy G.
Imperial College School of Medicine	Oliver M.
Industrial Development Board	Fleming L.
Industry Council for Packaging and the Environment	Bickerstagge J.
Institute of Human Nutrition	Jackson A.
Institute for Animal Health	Bostock C.
Institute of Agricultural Medicine and Rehabilitation	Gard R.
Institute of Arable Crops Research	James S.
Institute of Biology	Cowie J.
Institute of Food Research	Malcom A.
Institute of Food Science and Technology	Wild H.
Institute of Human Nutrition	Margetts B.
Institute of Professionals, Managers and Specialists	Ellis V.
Institute of Trading Standards Administration	Greaty G.
Institution of Chemical Engineers	Barber A.
International Agency for Cancer Research	Riboli E.
International Federation of Environmental Health	Halls M.
Ipswich Borough Council	Park C.
Isle of Wight Council	Appleby D.
Kelloggs UK	Fletcher R.
Kent Chief Environmental Health Officers Group	Hannan M.
Kettering Borough Council	Smith P.
King's College, London	Nelson M.
Kings Healthcare	Peters T.
Kingston Upon Hull City Council	Deeming J.
Kirklees Metropolitan Council	Russell J.
Laboratory of the Government Chemist	Worswick R.

Organisation	Name
LACOTS	Humble J.
Lanarkshire Health Board	Ahmed S.
Lancashire County Council	Lord D.
Lancashire County Council	Potts J.
Lancaster City Council	Robinson D
Leatherhead Food RA	Kierstan M.
Leeds City Council	Mepham P.
Leeds Health Authority	Scott L.
Leicester City Council	Statham D.
Leicestershire Health Authority'	Monk P.
Lewes District Council	Kedge I.
Lichfield District Council	Bratt R.
Limarady Borough Council	Rankin J.
Lincoln City Council	Hartford R.
Lisburn Borough Council	Woods M.
Liverpool Health Authority	Regan C.
Livestock Auctioneers Association	Martin J.
Local Government Association/LACOTS	Ryan J.
Lomond Healthcare NHS Trust	Dancer S.
London Borough of Barking and Dagenham	Payne R.
London Borough of Enfield	Steward M.
London Borough of Greenwich	Scott K.
London Borough of Harrow	Potts K.
London Food Study Group	Ramm S.
London School of Hygiene and Tropical Medicine	Shetty P.
Lothian Anti-Poverty Alliance	Scott B.
Lothian Health	Zealley H.
Luton Borough Council	Churchill J.
Maidstone Borough Council	Hatcher K.
Malt Distillers Association of Scotland	Grigor C. Young
Malvern Hills District Council	Seabright F.
Marks & Spencer	McCracken P.
Martello Associates	Duncan A.
Maryvale Farms	Gourlay S.
Mater Hospital	Wyatt T.
McDonalds Restaurants Ltd	Foster V.
Meat and Livestock Commission	Maclean C.
Meat Hygiene Service	McNeoll J.
Medical Research Council	Bridges B.
Medical Research Council	Coggon D.
Medical Research Council	Radda G.
Medicines Commission	Lawson D.
Mid Beds District Council	Byles C.
Middlesbrough Borough Council	Johnson O.

Organisation	Name
Milk for Schools	Spiers S.
Milk Quality Forum	Peacock B.
Mole Valley District Council	Tiffney J.
Moray Council	Summers J.
Moray Council	Connell A.
Moy Park	Thom I.
National Association of Agricultural Contractors	Hartle R.
National Association of British and Irish Millers	Murray J.
National Association of British Market Authorities	Zasada K.
National Association of Master Bakers	Dabner C.
National Consumer Council	Johnstone J.
National Council of Women	Nedekind G.
National Dairy Council	Stacey A.
National Dairymen's Association	Moxon A.
National Farmers Union	Gardiner I.
National Farmers Union of Scotland	Not Stated
National Federation of Consumer Groups	Gale B.
National Federation of Meat & Food Traders	Fuller J.
National Federation of Women's Institutes	Carey H.
National Heart Forum	Sharp I.
National Institute for Biological Standards and Control	Stewart R.
National Market Traders Federation	Burton J.
National Office of Animal health	Cook R.
National Radiological Protection Board	Dry F.
Neath Port Talbot County Borough Council	Bolchover S.
Nestlé	Hams D.
New Forest District Council	Stopher J.
Newcastle and North Tyneside Health Authority	Harvey J.
Newcastle University	Blain P.
Newry and Mourne District Council	O'Neill H.
Norfolk County Council	Barnard J.
North and East Devon Health Authority	Kealy M.
North Ayrshire Council	Bale S.
North Down Borough Council	Yarr D.
North East Derbyshire District Council	Foley P.
North East Lincolnshire Council	Oxby R.
North Lanarkshire Council	Robertson M.
North Lincolnshire Council	Clarke P.
North Nottingham Health	Williams D.
North of Ireland Veterinary Association	O'Brien J.
North Tyneside Council	Davison S.
North Warwickshire Borough Council	Staveley P.
North Yorkshire County Council	Gresty G.
Northamptonshire County Council	Wire T.

Organisation	Name
Northern Ireland Forum for Political Dialogue	Campbell R.
Northern Foods	Southgate R.
Northern Ireland Chief Environmental Health Officers Group	Not Stated
Northern Ireland Dairy Association	Shillington J.
Northern Ireland Food and Drink Association	Bell M.
Northern Ireland Meat Exporters Association	Mathers T.
Northern Ireland Public Service Alliance	McCusker J.
Northern Milk Partnership	Smith J.
Northumberland Health Authority	Singleton S.
Norwich City Council	Morrey B.
Norwich Research Park Association	Not Stated
Norwich University	Coll E.
Nottingham Health Authority	Slack R.
Nottingham University	Wartes W.
Nutrition Works	Hunt P.
Oldham Borough Council	Brown L.
Omagh District Council	Harte G.
OP Information Network	Sigmund E.
Oswestry Borough Council	Jones H.
Oxfordshire County Council	Yendale B.
Oxfordshire Health Authority	Mayon-White R.
Paterson Inst. for Cancer Research	Dexter T.
Pembrokeshire County Council	Seal D.
Pentland Management Consultants	Pentland H.
Perfecta Food Ingredients	Roberts P.
Perth and Kinross Council	Lewis E.
Perth and Kinross Council	Milne J.
Pet Food Manufacturers Association	Francis-Roberts L.
Pharmalink Associates	Wishart D.
PHLS, Nottingham	Wale M.
Plymouth City Council	Studden M.
Plymouth Hospitals NHS Trust	Thomas A.
Preston Borough Council	Garrity K.
Private individual	Atwood B.
Private individual	Barratt R.
Private individual	Beishan J.
Private individual	Blake A.
Private individual	Brady S.
Private individual	Bremner M.
Private individual	Brogan R.
Private individual	Burke D.
Private individual	Clayton K.
Private individual	Clegg F.
Private individual	Collins D.

Organisation	Name
Private individual	Collins O.
Private individual	Craig D.
Private individual	Cuthbertson W.
Private individual	Davidson J.
Private individual	Davies T.
Private individual	Denner W.
Private individual	Dibben C.
Private individual	Edwards B.
Private individual	Fallens J.
Private individual	Fore H.
Private individual	Georgala D.
Private individual	Hannant G.
Private individual	Hardinge A.
Private individual	Hawkins B.
Private individual	Hiltunen M.
Private individual.	Huntington P.
Private individual	Innes S.
Private individual	Jackson P.
Private individual	Jefferson A.
Private individual	Kimbell H.
Private individual	Kitchener
Private individual	Lawrence M.
Private individual	Lewis E.
Private individual	Lim G.
Private individual	Lockley R.
Private individual	Mackay D.
Private individual	Maddocks A.
Private individual	McLennan J.
Private individual	McWeeny D.
Private individual.	Micklewood P.
Private individual	Millar J.
Private individual	Miller D.
Private individual	Miller T.
Private individual	Moseley B.
Private individual	North R.
Private individual	Parkins B.
Private individual	Pigott G.
Private individual	Price H.
Private individual	Ramsay C.
Private individual	Ramsden E.
Private individual	Robertson B.
Private individual	Robertson M.
Private individual	Royle M.
Private individual	Saunders B.

Organisation	Name
Private individual	Saunders C.
Private Individual	Schofield G.
Private individual	Schweizer M.
Private individual	Shaw S.
Private individual	Simmons N.
Private individual	Sluce P.
Private individual	Smart J.
Private individual	Smith D.
Private individual	Southgate D.
Private individual	Steek J.
Private individual	Stiff P.
Private individual	Strong R.
Private individual	Tamlit M.
Private individual	Thomson J.
Private individual	Tucker M.
Private individual	Watson D.
Private individual	Whitaker J.
Product Assurance	Windibank R.
Proprietary Association of Great Britain	Smith E.
Public Health Laboratory Service	Duerden B.
Public Health Laboratory Service (Anglia and Oxford)	Willcocks L.
Public Health Medicine Environmental Group	Haworth E.
Queen Mary and Westfield College	Dayan A.
Queens University Belfast	Bundy T.
Reading Scientific Services	Gutteridge C.
Reading University	Williams R.
Redcar and Cleveland Borough Council	Thomson D.
Reindeer Foods Ltd	Cogman D.
Renfrewshire Council	Forteath B.
Renfrewshire Council	Smith C.
Rhondda-Cynon-Taff County Borough Council	Miles A.
River Tees Port Health Authority	Milner S.
Rochdale Metropolitan Borough Council	Hyndman J.
Rochford District Council	Woolhouse G.
Rother District Council	Mayson C.
Rotherham Borough Council	Stinson G.
Royal Alexandra Hospital	Williams C.
Royal Association of British Dairy Farmers	Gilbert P.
Royal College of Anaesthetists	Prys-Roberts C.
Royal College of Nursing	Hancock C.
Royal College of Obstetricians & Gynaecologists	Patel N.
Royal College of Paediatrics and Child Health	Dodd K.
Royal College of Pathologists	Roberts C.
Royal College of Physicians	Harling K.

Organisation	Name
Royal College of Psychiatrists	Kendell R.
Royal College of Veterinary Surgeons	Hern J.
Royal Environmental Health Institute — Scotland	Frater J.
Royal Highland and Agricultural Society of Scotland	Moyes C.
Royal Infirmary of Edinburgh	Swainson C.
Royal Institute of Public Health & Hygiene	Smith R.
Royal Kingston Borough Council	Smart R.
Royal Society	Collins P.
Royal Society of Chemistry	Benn S.
Royal Society of Health	Robert-Sargeant S.
Royal Veterinary College	Johnston A.
Royal Welsh Agricultural Society	Walters D.
Ruddock and Sherratt	Walker M.
Runnymede Borough Council	Holmes R.
Ryedale District Council	Oldridge S.
S.A.F.E. Alliance	Hird V.
Safeway	Handton B.
Safeway Stores plc	Combes T.
Sainsburys	Matthews N.
Salford City Council	Jassi M.
Sandwell Health Authority	Blair I.
Scientists for Labour	Mellon F.
Scotch Whisky Association	Hedley J.
Scottish Agricultural College	Thomas P.
Scottish Agricultural Organisation Society	Brown E.
Scottish Centre for Infection and Environmental Health	Campbell D.
Scottish Centre for Infection and Environmental Health	Reilly W.
Scottish Consumer Council	Foster A.
Scottish Crop Research Institute	Hillman J.
Scottish Environment Protection Agency	Menton M.
Scottish Federation of Meat Traders Associations	Booden R.
Scottish Fish Merchant's Federation	Milne R.
Scottish Food Co-ordinating Committee	McDonald C.
Scottish Grocers Federation	Jamie R.
Scottish Meat Wholesalers	Stevenson J.
Scottish Safety Officers Registration Board	Houston C.
Seafish Industry Authority	Chaplin P.
Sheffield City Council	MGrogan G.
Sheffield Hallam University	Salfield
Shropshire County Council	Walker D.
Slough Borough Council	Francis A.
Slough Borough Council	Cutting G.
Society of Chief Officers of Environmental Health in Scotland	Evans D.
Society of Directors of Public Protection, Wales	Lumley J.

Organisation	Name
Society of Environmental Health	Cooper S.
Society of Food Hygiene Technology	Stephens A.
Society of Local Authority Chief Executives	Cole M.
Society of Public Health	Gardner P.
Soil Association	Holden P.
Somerset County Council Scientific Services	Stephenson G.
Somerset County Council Solicitors Dept	Whitrutt J.
Somerset County Council Trading Standards	Whitanst J.
South Ayrshire Council	Collier B.
South Gloucestershire Council	Latimer K.
South Hams District Council	Bloomer J.
South Humber Health Authority	Hill T.
South Norfolk Council	Durell T.
South Tyneside Metropolitan Borough Council	McQueen F.
Southern Derbyshire Health Authority	Newlands M.
Southern Group Environmental Health Committee	Joyce M.
Southern Health and Social Services Board	Cunningham B.
Specialist Cheesemakers Association	Cunynghame A.
St Ann's Hospital Poole	Lay C.
St. Bartholomew's & Royal London School of Medicine & Dentistry	Berry C.
St. Helens & Knowsley Health Authority	Wiratunga E.
Stevenage Borough Council	Harrington L.
Stirling Council	Fisher L.
Stockton-on-Tees Borough Council	Francis D.
Stoke on Trent City Council	Ward B.
Strachan Associates	Strachan P.
Strathaird Quality Seafoods	Hunter J.
Strathclyde University	Jackson M.
Stroud District Council	May K.
Sugar Bureau	Sutcliffe J.
Surrey University	O'Brien J.
Sutton Environmental Services	Everett T.
Swindon Borough Council	Lewis L.
Tandridge District Council	Thomas P.
TAS International	Tennant D.
Tayside Health Board	Barrie L.
Tayside Health Board Health Promotion Centre	Woodcock A.
Teignbridge Environmental Health	Hosford B.
Tesco	Longworth J.
Toxoplasmosis Trust	Asbury C.
Transport and General Workers Union	Morris B.
Tunbridge Wells Borough Council	Stock D.
Tynedale Council	Darling I.
UK Agricultural Supply Trade Association	Reed J.

Organisation	Name
UK Association of Frozen Food Producers	Molloy G.
UK Egg Producers Association	Pulman K.
UK Federation of Milk Producer Organisations	Jones D.
UK Provision Trade Federation	Cheney C.
Ulster Farmers Union	Aston W.
Ulster University	Smith T.
Unigate	Buckland R.
Unilever	Walker W.
Unilever	Schofield G.
Unison	Sonnet K.
United Biscuits	Little M.
United Dairy Farmers	Agnew S.
United Kingdom Register of Organic Food Standards	Spedding C.
University College London	Marmot M.
University College London — Medical School	Pattison J.
University College London — Medical School	Brunner E.
University of Aberdeen	Pennington T.
University of Aberdeen	Little J.
University of East Anglia	O'Riordan T.
University of Glasgow	Lean M.
University of Glasgow	Wright N.
University of Newcastle	Ritson C.
University of Sheffield	Woods H.
University of Surrey	O'Brien J.
University of Wales Institute Cardiff	Griffith C.
University of Wales Swansea	Parry J.
University of York	Garnder R.
Vale of the White Horse Council	Sadler T.
Vegetarian Economy and Green Agriculture	Long A.
Vegetarian Society	Fox T.
Verner Wheelock Associates	Wheelock V.
Veterinary Products Committee	Aitken I.
Veterinary Public Health Association	Huey P.
Wandsworth Council	Avery J.
Warwickshire County Council	Hunter N.
Wellsprings Confectionery Ltd.	Price G.
Welsh Collaboration for Health and Environment	Hall R.
Welsh Consumer Council	Brookes B.
Welsh Food Alliance	Smith D.
Wessex Institute for Health Research & Development	Margetts B.
West Devon Borough Council	Payne N.
West Glasgow Hospitals University Trust	Bryson A.
West Kent Health Authority	Hean Ang. L.
West Lothian Council	Campbell A.

Organisation	Name
West Pennine Health Authority	Lighton L.
West Surrey Health Authority	Simpson J.
West Wiltshire District Council	Bardwell D.
West Yorkshire Trading Standards Service	Wood M.
Western General Hospitals Trust	Hanson M.
Western Health and Social Services Board	Smithson R.
Westminster Council	Kemp P.
Whitbread	Miller T.
Winchester City Council	Boardman D.
Woking Borough Council	Smith B.
Wolfson Institute of Preventative Medicine	Ward N.
Women's Environment Network	Steinbrecher R.
Women's Farming Union	Kerdall S.
Women's Farming Union	Stroude M.
Women's Farming Union	Collingham R.
Women's National Commission	Davis P.
Worcester Community Services Department	Fidoe R.
Worcestershire Health Authority	Tweddall A.
Worthing Borough Council	Bowen D.
York City Council	Haswell R.

Includes responses received after the end of the consultation period

Annex 2 :
The existing arrangements

1. This Annex outlines the current administrative arrangements for handling food safety and standards in the UK, as well as the legislative background to these areas of policy.

UK legislation

2. The Food Safety Act 1990 constitutes the main framework for food legislation in Great Britain. The Government endorses Professor James's observation that it is generally recognised to be an effective tool for promoting food safety. The Act, of which the main provisions came into force on 1 January 1991, comprehensively revises and consolidates a variety of existing controls on food safety. Northern Ireland has equivalent legislation.

3. Other main pieces of primary legislation that relate to food safety and standards and provide Ministers with a wide range of powers and controls on the production, distribution, handling and sale of food, are listed in Appendix 1 to this Annex. This Appendix is intended to be a general guide to the principal legislation relating to food safety and standards, and is not an exhaustive list of all relevant powers.

EC food law

4. The great majority of secondary legislation concerning food in the UK derives from rules that are agreed in EU negotiations. Close liaison with the European institutions and with other member states of the European Union will clearly constitute an important element of the Agency's work (Chapter 3 considers the EU and international role of the Agency in detail).

5. EC food law has been built up in a new framework since the mid-1980s, when the European Commission decided that efforts to harmonise Member States' national rules on the composition and labelling of food should be redirected towards agreeing new ''horizontal'' rules that could apply across the board to all or most foods. The main horizontal directives cover food additives, labelling, contaminants, food contact materials, foods for particular nutritional uses, and food law enforcement. While there are a number of food hygiene directives that relate to specific products, for example meat, fish and milk, there is also a horizontal directive on the general hygiene of foodstuffs, covering all products that are not of animal origin and the retailing and catering of all foodstuffs. There are in addition directives and regulations which deal with specific food safety related matters such as irradiation, novel foods and lot marking.

Departmental Responsibilities

6. At present, the Ministry of Agriculture, Fisheries and Food (MAFF) has the lead responsibility for issues concerning food standards, chemical safety of food, food labelling, food technology and meat and milk hygiene. The Department of Health (DH) takes the lead on food hygiene, microbiological food safety and nutrition. The Scottish Office, Welsh Office and the Northern Ireland Department of Health and Social Services have responsibility for food issues within their geographical areas.

7. Lead Departments take primary responsibility for developing policy on issues within their remit, for reporting on those issues to Parliament and for preparing legislation. In practice, Departments and Agencies liaise closely with each other to ensure that policy and legislation are developed coherently.

8. To assist it in the execution of its policies, MAFF is served by a number of Executive Agencies responsible for discrete areas of work that are relevant to food safety. These are the Veterinary Medicines Directorate, the Pesticides Safety Directorate, the Meat Hygiene Service, the Veterinary Laboratories Agency (which provides veterinary advice based on investigation and surveillance), the Central Science Laboratory (which provides scientific services in support of a wide range of the Ministry's food policies), and the

Farming and Rural Conservation Agency (whose Dairy Hygiene Inspectorate enforces the dairy hygiene legislation on farms in England and Wales).

9. Ministers and Departments are supported in their work by a range of Advisory Committees, whose role is to provide independent expert advice on particular areas of work. In addition, MAFF provides the secretariat to the Consumer Panel, a group of independent lay and consumer representatives who meet four times a year to discuss the Government's food policies. Details of the main expert and Advisory Committees dealing with food issues are given in Appendix 2.

Enforcement Responsibilities

10. The great majority of food law enforcement is carried out by local authorities (LAs). The only exceptions to this are enforcement of certain provisions on meat hygiene and inspection, and part of the milk hygiene regulations in England and Wales, which are carried out by Executive Agencies of MAFF (see below). In addition certain enforcement activities in Northern Ireland are undertaken by DANI.

11. Local authorities have a duty to enforce food law made under the Food Safety Act 1990. They are responsible for initiating prosecutions under the Act and for investigating complaints that are passed on by consumers. Local authority inspectorates are free to choose the most appropriate manner of enforcement, working to Central Government guidance published in codes of practice.

12. Enforcement is carried out by Trading Standards Officers (TSOs) and Environmental Health Officers (EHOs). Both have a wide range of duties with some overlap in the food area. TSOs cover legislation on food standards and labelling, including quality, composition, presentation and advertising of food, materials in contact with food, weights and measures, consumer credit, consumer safety, animal movements and animal feedingstuffs. EHOs are responsible for work on food hygiene (including food safety and microbiological contamination) as well as safety at work, housing, pollution and noise. TSO and EHO functions are carried out by separate inspectorates in England, but are combined in a single department in most Welsh local authorities.

13. In Scotland and Northern Ireland, enforcement of all aspects of legislation on food standards and labelling and food safety and hygiene are the responsibility of Environmental Health Departments, in the single tier authorities. Generally EHOs are responsible for food law enforcement.

14. Surveillance of the microbiological safety of food is carried out in England and Wales by the Public Health Laboratory Service (PHLS) on behalf of local environmental health departments, the Department of Health and the Welsh Office. The PHLS has around fifty local laboratories, all with special facilities for the microbiological examination of food. In addition there are other specialised laboratories providing a range of microbiological services. The PHLS also provides information to physicians in general practice.

15. In Scotland, surveillance of the safety of food is carried out by local authorities, co-ordinated by the Scottish Food Co-ordinating Committee. There is no PHLS in Scotland and microbiological food examinations are undertaken by a number of local authority, NHS Trust and independent private laboratories. Specialist laboratory services are provided by reference laboratories and other laboratories funded directly by the Scottish Office.

16. In Northern Ireland, Environmental Health Officers send samples of food taken for microbiological examination to the Public Health Laboratory at Belfast City Hospital. The surveillance is co-ordinated by the Food Liaison Group of the Northern Ireland Chief Environmental Health Officers' Group.

17. Local authorities are required to appoint Public Analysts who are qualified and equipped

to carry out the chemical analysis required for compositional sampling work under the Food Safety Act 1990. There are thirty one Public Analysts' laboratories in the UK, over half of which are based within local authority departments. The remainder are private laboratories appointed as Public Analysts by local authorities.

18. Port health authorities are responsible for enforcing controls on food imported from countries outside the European Union.

19. In England and Wales local authority enforcement is co-ordinated by the Local Authorities Co-ordinating Body on Food and Trading Standards (LACOTS), which provides advice and guidance to local authorities on enforcement issues. The Scottish Food Co-ordinating Committee (SFCC) carries out a similar role in Scotland, although LACOTS also extends to Scotland and Northern Ireland. Along with the Local Government Association, both offer advice and comment to Central Government on enforcement. In Northern Ireland the district councils outside Belfast have come together to form four groups. Those, together with Belfast, play a co-ordinating role on enforcement.

20. The Meat Hygiene Service (MHS) was established in April 1995 as an Executive Agency of MAFF. It is the central authority responsible for meat hygiene and inspection functions that were formerly exercised by local authorities. The MHS enforces hygiene and welfare laws in licensed slaughterhouses through Official Veterinary Surgeons assisted by Meat Hygiene Inspectors. The service is audited by the Veterinary Public Health Unit of the Joint Food Safety and Standards Group, acting in its own right and on behalf of the Chief Veterinary Officer. The State Veterinary Service carries out a separate audit of compliance with the specified risk material legislation. In Northern Ireland DANI is responsible for meat hygiene and inspection services.

21. Enforcement of milk hygiene standards (up to, but not including, pasteurisation and bottling) at registered (farm) holdings is undertaken by the Dairy Hygiene Inspectorate of the Farming and Rural Conservation Agency (FRCA) on behalf of MAFF and the Welsh Office. Enforcement of other aspects of milk hygiene legislation in approved establishments (including pasteurisation and bottling) is controlled by local authorities, usually Environmental Health Departments. In Scotland, all milk hygiene enforcement is carried out by local authorities. In Northern Ireland the Department of Agriculture fulfils the role of the FRCA in England and Wales.

Food Safety Act 1990

1.   This Act is the main piece of primary food legislation in GB. The Act is principally an enabling piece of legislation but it also provides for offences and defences in law and defines food and the enforcement authorities and their responsibilities. It also provides Ministers with various powers. The main provisions of the Food Safety Act 1990 came into force on 1 January 1991. The Act covers Great Britain and provides the framework for all its food legislation. Northern Ireland has equivalent legislation, the Food Safety (Northern Ireland) Order 1991, which came into force on 21 May 1991.

The Food And Environment Protection Act 1985

2.   Part I of the Act empowers Ministers to make emergency orders where they consider that circumstances exist, or may exist, which are likely to create a hazard to human health through the consumption of contaminated food. Such orders prohibit the distribution of affected produce from an area where foodstuffs have, or may have, been contaminated. In practice these powers are used only where there are no other statutory means of dealing with contaminated food (e.g. sector-specific legislation under the Food Safety Act 1990).

3.   Part I of the Food and Environment Protection Act was amended by Section 51 of the Food Safety Act 1990. The Act also applies in Scotland, Wales and Northern Ireland.

4.   Part III of the Act governs control of pesticides, conferring on Ministers powers to control the importation, sale, supply, storage, use and advertisement of pesticides and to set maximum pesticide residue levels in food, crops and feedingstuffs, to make information on pesticides available to the public, and to enforce these provisions and to establish an Advisory Committee on pesticides.

The Weights And Measures Act 1985

5.   Section 28 of the 1985 Act makes short weight an offence. Orders made under Section 22 require prepacked food to carry on the container an indication of the net quantity of the contents. When sold other than prepacked, food is required either to be sold by quantity or, in certain circumstances, the seller has to make the quantity known to the customer. Orders also limit the quantities in which certain goods (the prescribed quantity goods) may be prepacked when offered for retail sale. Northern Ireland has equivalent legislation, the Weights and Measures (Northern Ireland) Order 1981.

The Trade Descriptions Act 1968

6.   This Act makes it an offence for a person acting in the course of a trade or business to make false or misleading statements about goods, or knowingly or recklessly to make false or misleading statements about services, accommodation or facilities. It contains Order-making powers to require that goods bear, or be accompanied by specific information in the course of their supply, and to define terms for the purposes of the Act. The Act prohibits the unauthorised use of devices or emblems signifying Royal approval or award. The Act also applies in Scotland and Northern Ireland.

The Consumer Protection Act 1987

7.   Part I imposes civil liability for damage caused by defective products (including food other than game and agricultural produce which has not been subjected to an industrial process). Part II provides for secondary legislation on consumer safety, e.g. of materials in contact with food.

8.   Part III makes it an offence for a consumer to be given a misleading indication, by any means, of the price at which goods are available. Guidance is contained in The Code of Practice for Traders on Price Indications. The Act also contains powers to regulate specific price indications practices. Northern Ireland has equivalent legislation, the

Consumer Protection (Northern Ireland) Order 1987.

The Animal Health Act 1981

9. This Act confers on Ministers powers to control diseases of animals, including power to make Zoonoses Orders to reduce the risk to human health from any disease of, or organism carried in animals, (e.g. brucellosis, salmonella and BSE), to control the use of animal waste and by-products in relation to animal feedingstuffs, and to enable surveillance of live animals on-farm.

The Agriculture Act 1970 (as amended)

10. Part IV governs fertilisers and animal feedingstuffs and requires that feedingstuffs when sold should be fit for their intended purpose and free from harmful ingredients. A statutory statement is required on the composition of the feed and other information. Regulations made under the above Act cover Great Britain. Northern Ireland has separate but parallel secondary legislation made under the Act.

Agriculture And Horticulture Act 1964 (Chapter 28 Part III)

11. This Act provides for the application and enforcement in Great Britain of European Community Regulations specifying the grading, marketing and labelling requirements for certain fresh fruit and vegetables and makes certain acts or omissions that contravene those rules punishable offences. Northern Ireland has equivalent legislation, the Horticulture Act (Northern Ireland) 1966.

International Carriage of Perishable Foodstuffs Act 1976

12. This Act enables Regulations to be made governing the standards for transport equipment used for the international carriage of perishable foodstuffs.

Agricultural Produce (Grading and Marking) Acts 1928-31

13. This Act enables Regulations to be made concerning the grading and marking of agricultural produce and the cold storage of eggs.

Radioactive Substances Act 1993

14. This Act controls the disposal of radioactive waste.

Environmental Protection Act 1990

15. Part VI of the Act aims to prevent or minimise damage to the environment caused by the release of genetically modified organisms, and imposes restrictions on the importation, acquisition, release or marketing of such organisms.

The Medicines Act 1968

16. This Act controls the manufacture and marketing of medicinal products for humans and animals. It enables Regulations to be made implementing European Council Directive 90/167/EEC concerning the preparation, placing on the market and use of medicated animal feedingstuffs. The Act also applies in Scotland and Northern Ireland.

The Prices Act 1974

17. This Act enables Regulations to be made requiring prices to be displayed on any premises where food and drink is or may be for sale for consumption by the public. The Act also applies in Scotland and Northern Ireland.

Alcoholic Liquor Duties Act 1979

18. Section 71 prescribes a penalty for misdescribing liquor as spirits or as wine fortified with spirits. In practice, therefore, this Section reinforces Section 15 of the Food Safety Act 1990 as far as these products are concerned. The Act also applies in Scotland and Northern Ireland.

Scotch Whisky Act 1988

19. The Scotch Whisky Act 1988 makes provision as to the definition of Scotch Whisky and production and sale of whisky. Northern Ireland has equivalent legislation, the Scotch Whisky (Northern Ireland) Order 1988.

Public Health (Control of Disease) Act 1984

20. Regulations made under Part II (Control of Disease) enable local authorities to impose controls to prevent the spread of food poisoning and food-borne infections in persons involved in the food trade.

Public Health (Scotland) Acts 1897 to 1907

21. Sections 58 and 59 prohibit infected persons engaging in any occupation connected with food unless proper precautions have been taken against spreading disease or infection.

European Communities Act 1972

22. Section 2(2) of the European Communities Act makes provision for any designated Minister or Department to make regulations for the purpose of implementing any European Community obligations of the United Kingdom.

Role and Structure

1.　Advisory Committees exist to provide advice to Ministers and to other Advisory Committees on matters where an independent expert opinion is required. Some of the Committees are set up on a statutory basis. Others are non-statutory. All of the Committees publish reports.

2.　Committee Members are appointed for their expertise in a particular field. Many of the Committees which advise Health and Agriculture Ministers have a mainly scientific membership because of the nature of the issues to be considered by them. However, most of the Committees already have at least one 'lay member' to put forward the point of view of the consumer. Those which do not are currently in the process of appointing lay members.

3.　Advisory Committees may also seek the advice of one another on an ad hoc basis. For example, the Advisory Committee on Novel Foods and Processes may seek the advice of the Committee on Toxicity of Chemicals in Foods, Consumer Products and the Environment (COT) on specific toxicological issues. Cross-membership of Committees also exists in a great many cases. This helps to keep committees up-to-date with the thinking and opinions of other committees.

4.　There are also a number of Working Parties which advise Health and Agriculture Ministers and the Joint Food Safety and Standards Group on its surveillance programmes.

5.　A list of the principal Advisory Committees which advise Health and Agriculture Ministers on food and food-related issues and their remits follows.

ADVISORY COMMITTEE ON THE MICROBIOLOGICAL SAFETY OF FOOD (ACMSF) Non-statutory.

ACMSF is a broadly based committee which advises Ministers on the risks to humans of micro-organisms which are used or occur in food, and on the exercise of powers in the Food Safety Act 1990 relating to the microbiological safety of food. It is responsible for advising on the Government's microbiological food surveillance programme and its findings, and undertakes investigations into specific areas of microbiological interest/risk. When the ACMSF publishes a report containing advice to Government and others, the Government's response is published simultaneously.

ADVISORY COMMITTEE ON NOVEL FOODS AND PROCESSES (ACNFP) Non-statutory.

ACNFP advises Ministers on any matters relating to the irradiation of food, and the manufacture of novel foods including genetically modified foods and foods produced by novel processes. It takes advice from specialist committees where relevant. It considers specific applications from the food industry made under the EC Regulations on novel foods and novel food ingredients and advises Ministers on whether they should be cleared, and publishes specific reports when clearances are given for individual novel foods and processes, as well as an annual report.

ADVISORY COMMITTEE ON PESTICIDES (ACP) Statutory.

The ACP was put on a legal basis by Schedule 5 of the Food and Environmental Protection Act 1985. The Act states that the Ministers shall consult the ACP as to regulations which they contemplate making, as to approvals which they contemplate giving, revoking or suspending and as to conditions to which they contemplate making approvals subject. ACP publishes evaluation documents of new active ingredients and reviewed products, as well as an annual report.

COMMITTEE ON MEDICAL ASPECTS OF FOOD AND NUTRITION POLICY (COMA) Non-statutory.

COMA considers and advises Ministers on the medical and scientific aspects of nutrition and developments in the agricultural and food industries. It reports to the CMO as well as being chaired by him and publishes annual and specific reports. COMA has two study panels to advise on Maternal and Child Nutrition and Novel Foods. It also convenes expert Working Groups to report on specific issues (e.g. cardiovascular disease, cancer). These are disbanded after they report.

COMMITTEE ON MEDICAL ASPECTS OF RADIATION IN THE ENVIRONMENT (COMARE) Non-statutory.

COMARE's terms of Reference are "to assess and advise Government on the health effects of natural and man-made radiation in the environment and to assess the adequacy of the available data and the need for further research". It publishes specific reports on issues on which it is asked to advise.

COMMITTEE ON TOXICITY OF CHEMICALS IN FOOD, CONSUMER PRODUCTS AND THE ENVIRONMENT (COT) Non-statutory.

COT is a specialist committee, with a significant proportion of its work on toxicity relating to food safety issues. It reports to the CMO and through him to Ministers. It gives advice on additives in food once a 'case of need' has been established by the FAC. It also advises the ACNFP on Toxicological Safety. It publishes an annual report and specific reports.

THE COMMITTEE ON CARCINO-GENICITY and THE COMMITTEE ON MUTAGENICITY

are equivalent committees to COT which advise on these specific aspects of toxicology. Food-related topics represent a smaller proportion of their work.

CONSUMER PANEL Non-statutory.

The Consumer Panel comprises individuals nominated in a personal capacity by leading consumer organisations. Their role is to represent the views of ordinary consumers to Ministers on food issues of concern to consumers, and to advise on the transparency of food policies and on the transmission of advice and information on food safety, diet and nutrition. It publishes all agendas, minutes and discussion papers, plus an annual report.

FOOD ADVISORY COMMITTEE (FAC) Non-statutory.

FAC is a broadly based committee which advises Ministers on matters relating to the labelling, composition and chemical safety of food. Its task is to review and prepare reports on all matters within its remit. It takes advice from relevant expert committees (e.g. food chemical toxicology from COT) and its membership includes the chairman of COT. It has recently taken on responsibility for the oversight of the food surveillance programme. It publishes an annual report and reports on specific investigations.

SPONGIFORM ENCEPHALOPATHY ADVISORY COMMITTEE (SEAC) Non-statutory.

SEAC advises Government on all matters relating to BSE and CJD. It considers the implications of research findings for public and animal health, and recommends possible action and further research. Its advice to Government on specific issues is published.

VETERINARY PRODUCTS COMMITTEE (VPC) Statutory

The VPC was created under Section 4 of the Medicines Act 1968. Its remit is to give advice to the Licensing Authority (Agriculture and Health Ministers) with respect to safety, quality and efficacy in relation to the veterinary use of any substance or article to which the Medicines Act

applies, and to promote the collection of information relating to suspected adverse reactions. It publishes an Annual Report and a specific report following each monthly meeting.

Glossary

ACMSF	Advisory Committee on the Microbiological Safety of Food.
ACNFP	Advisory Committee on Novel Foods and Processes.
ACP	Advisory Committee on Pesticides.
ADAS	Formerly an Executive Agency of MAFF and the Welsh Office, ADAS (previously known as the Agricultural Development Advisory Service) was privatised on 1 April 1997. It provides technical, strategic and business consultancy to all land based industries, especially food production, processing and retailing, land management, waste disposal and energy. The Farming and Rural Conservation Agency (FRCA) now carries out those functions of ADAS which were not considered suitable for privatisation.
Advisory Committees	See Annex 2, Appendix 2.
Aflatoxins	A group of mycotoxins produced by moulds which grow in improperly stored nuts, grains, dried fruits and certain other foods.
BBSRC	Biotechnology and Biological Sciences Research Council.
Better Regulation Guide	Produced by the Better Regulation Unit, Cabinet Office in 1997. This guide describes good practice at all stages of regulating including guidance, using a worked example, on the preparation of Regulatory Appraisals.
BSE	Bovine Spongiform Encephalopathy is a neurological disorder affecting adult cattle. It is a subacute transmissible spongiform encephalopathy and is believed to be the bovine equivalent of scrapie disease in sheep, that has occurred as the result of the exposure of cattle to animal feeds containing the scrapie agent.
CAP	Common Agricultural Policy. British agriculture policy has been integrated within the CAP since the UK joined the European Community in 1973. Its objectives are as follows:
	a) ensuring the rational development of agricultural production thus ensuring a fair standard of living for the agricultural population
	b) to stabilise markets
	c) to guarantee a secure supply of food
	d) to assure reasonable retail prices to consumers.
CCDC	Consultant in Communicable Disease Control.
Chief Medical Officer	The Chief Medical Officer is the professional head of the Medical Civil Service and the Department of Health medical staff. He is also the Chief Medical Officer for the Government, the Department for Education and Employment, MAFF, the Home Office and the

Department of Social Security. He also provides medical advice to other Government Departments including DETR, DTI and FCO. Territorial Departments each have their own CMO whose role is to advise their respective Secretary of State and other territorial ministers. They oversee the work of policy units in their respective Health Departments. Responsibilities include preparing and publishing an annual report on the health of the population. There is also an important liaison role between the Chief Medical Officers.

Chief Veterinary Officer

The Chief Veterinary Officer (CVO) is the professional head of the Veterinary Service and principal adviser to MAFF and other Whitehall Departments and their Ministers on veterinary matters. The CVO plays an important role in representing the United Kingdom in a wide range of international fora on issues related to the protection of public and animal health, the promotion of animal welfare and the facilitation of trade in animals and animal products. The CVO as head of the State Veterinary Service also has responsibility for ensuring that Government policy in these areas is fully implemented.

Codex Alimentarius

Latin for food code. It is a code of food standards for all nations, developed by an international commission established in 1962 when the FAO and the WHO recognised the need for international standards to guide the world's growing food industry and to protect the health of consumers. The standards contain "requirements for food aimed at ensuring the consumer a sound, wholesome food product free from adulteration and correctly labelled and presented".

COMA

Committee on Medical Aspects of Food and Nutrition Policy.

Commissioner for Public Appointments

Appointed by the Head of State to monitor, regulate and provide advice on Government Departments' procedures for Ministerial appointments to public bodies.

Communicable disease

A disease, the causative organisms of which are capable of being passed from a person, animal or the environment (which would include food and water) to a susceptible individual.

Competent authority

A body or institution which has the authority to enforce Commission legislation.

Compositional requirements

The minimum legal requirements for manufactured foods.

Council of Ministers

The Council is the only EU institution which directly represents the fifteen Member Governments, each Government holding a seat. The Council is the Communities' principal decision making body, acting on proposals from the European Commission.

Crown Office Holder	A person appointed to a civil office under the Crown, either by the Crown itself, or on behalf of the Crown by a Minister of the Crown, or in some cases by some non-ministerial office holders.
Deliberate Release	The intentional introduction into the environment of a genetically modified organism.
DETR	Department of the Environment, Transport and the Regions.
DH	Department of Health.
Dietary supplements sold as food	These are products which are generally sold in capsule, pill, powder or tablet form, which are intended to supplement the diet and which are not subject to licensing under medicines regulation.
Directives (horizontal and vertical)	Instruments of EC legislation. Vertical Directives regulate a specific commodity or industrial sector. Horizontal Directives regulate more than one commodity or industrial sector.
Directorate General	An administrative Department of the European Commission. There are currently 24 Directorate Generals.
DTI	Department of Trade and Industry.
Due diligence defence	Section 21 of the Food Safety Act 1990 introduced a due diligence defence into food law in GB. The provision can apply differently in different circumstances. Sub-section 1 applies generally. It provides a defence that the person charged took all reasonable precautions and exercised all due diligence to avoid the commission of the offence by himself or by a person under his control. This defence is available to manufacturers and to importers of the food as well as to retailers.
DWI	Drinking Water Inspectorate — reports to the Secretary of State for the Environment, Transport and the Regions and the Secretary of State for Wales. Main tasks are to carry out technical audits of water companies; advise the Secretary of State on the steps required to enforce obligations under the relevant legislation; investigate accidents which affect water quality adversely; advise on the prosecution of water companies if water has been supplied which is unfit for human consumption and to provide technical and scientific advice to Ministers and officials on drinking water policy issues including water quality, research and consumer complaints.
EC	European Community.
Enabling powers	Provisions in primary legislation conferring powers, usually on a Minister or Ministers, to make secondary legislation.
EU	European Union.
EU competence	Whereby the EU has legal authority to act.

Executive Agency	An executive agency is a Government Department, or semi-autonomous unit within a Department, which carries out executive functions within a policy and resources framework set by Ministers.
FAO	Food and Agriculture Organisation, a branch of the United Nations.
FRCA	Farming and Rural Conservation Agency. Provides services to the Government on the design, development and implementation of policies on the integration of farming and conservation, rural land use and diversification in the rural economy.
Food Hazard Warning System	A system operated by the Department of Health to alert local enforcement authorities, and where necessary, the EU to any foodborne risk to public health.
Fortified foods	Foods to which nutrients have been deliberately added.
FSA	Food Standards Agency.
Functional foods	Foods which claim to have special properties valuable to health, but which do not have a medicinal product licence.
GMO	Genetically Modified Organism. An organism in which the genetic material has been altered in a way that does not occur naturally by mating and/or natural recombination.
Grant-in-aid	This is a payment to a body to assist it in furthering its objectives.
HSC/HSE	Health and Safety Commission and Executive. Statutory bodies created under the Health and Safety at Work etc. Act 1974. Report primarily to the Secretary of State for the Environment, Transport and the Regions but also report to other Secretaries of State for certain functions. Responsible for ensuring that risks to peoples' health and safety from work activities are properly controlled.
Hygiene Assessment System (HAS)	A risk-based method of assessing hygiene standards in licensed slaughterhouses and cutting plants; generates the HAS score.
Integrated Pollution Prevention and Control	EC Directive 96/91 on Integrated Pollution Prevention and Control lays down measures designed to prevent, or where that is not practicable reduce, emissions to air, water and land from a range of the potentially most polluting industrial activities in order to achieve a high level of protection for the environment as a whole. The requirements of the directive must be transposed into UK legislation by 31 October 1999.
Irradiation	Food irradiation is exposure to ionising radiation resulting in a reduction in the levels of bacteria. It can also be used to kill pathogenic organisms, reduce spoilage and delay ripening and sprouting in food.
LACOTS	Local Authorities Co-ordinating Body on Food and Trading Standards is a local authority funded body created to promote good law and best

practice in trading standards and food safety. LACOTS is the Single Liaison Body for the United Kingdom.

Legislation (primary and secondary)	Primary legislation is laws enacted by Parliament, known as statutes or Acts of Parliament. In general, statutes contain major policy and legal provisions and often contain enabling powers for Ministers to make secondary legislation.

Secondary legislation is instruments made under powers conferred by, or under statute, the commonest forms of which are regulations and orders. |
LINK programmes	The LINK initiative promotes partnership between industry and the research base with the aim of stimulating innovation and wealth creation. LINK research, which is pre-competitive, covers a wide range of technology and generic product areas. MAFF supports several programmes of food research under the LINK scheme.
MAFF	Ministry of Agriculture, Fisheries and Food.
Medicines Control Agency	This is an Executive Agency of the Department of Health reporting to the Secretary of State. It deals with the implementation of the Medicines Acts 1968 and 1971 and the Biological Standards Act 1975. It also covers policy matters relating to the safety, quality and efficacy of medicines and international aspects of medicines control.
MRC	The Medical Research Council (MRC) is a research organisation which aims to improve health by promoting research into all areas of medical and related science. It supports medical research through its research establishments, grants to individual scientists and support for post-graduate students.
Mutual recognition arrangements	Mutual recognition is a procedure under which a pharmaceutical company, having obtained a marketing authorisation for its veterinary medicinal product in one member state, can apply to one or more of the other member states to recognise that approval and grant identical authorisations.
Natural toxicants	These are poisonous substances which occur naturally in a wide variety of foods. Consuming normal amounts of foods containing these substances causes no harm.
NDPB	A Non-Departmental Public Body is an organisation which has a role in the processes of national government, but is not a government department or part of one, and accordingly operates to a greater or lesser extent at arm's length from Ministers.
Next Steps	The Next Steps initiative was launched in 1988 to improve management in government by promoting general principles of good management, including accountability, delegation and openness.

Nolan principles	Are the general principles of conduct which underpin public life. These are selflessness, integrity, objectivity, accountability, openness, honesty and leadership.
Novel Foods and processes	A novel food is one which has not previously been used for human consumption to a significant degree in the EU.
Office of Science and Technology (OST)	Part of the Department of Trade and Industry; the OST's aim is to develop and co-ordinate, transdepartmentally, Government policy on science, engineering and technology.
Our Healthier Nation	The Government's new health strategy for England. A Green Paper for consultation is to be published this winter, leading to a White Paper for summer 1998.
Parliamentary Select Committee	A cross-party committee of MPs "selected" for a particular task, generally one of inquiry, investigation and scrutiny. Amongst the most common Parliamentary Select Committees are the departmentally-related Select Committees which examine the expenditure, administration and policy of government departments and associated public bodies.
Pathogen	Any micro-organism that causes a disease.
Peach rules	Govern Ministerial appointments to executive NDPB's and NHS bodies issued by the Commissioner for Public Appointments (Sir Len Peach). The rules are set out in detail in the Commissioner's *"Code of Practice for Public Appointments Procedures"*.
Peer review	The process used by the scientific community to assess a scientific paper, report, project, or proposal by seeking comments on it from independent assessors ('peers') working in the same field.
Pennington Report	The report of the Pennington Group on "the circumstances leading to the 1996 outbreak of infection with E.coli 0157 in Central Scotland, the implications for food safety and the lessons to be learned".
PHLS	The Public Health Laboratory Service — provides clinical diagnostic microbiology services to NHS Trusts, general practitioners and other customers, as well as food and environmental microbiology for public health customers, including health and local authorities. Its laboratories also assist health and local authorities in the investigation of outbreaks of infection, and contribute to the surveillance of communicable disease, locally and nationally.
PSD	Pesticides Safety Directorate, an Executive Agency of MAFF. The Directorate monitors and licenses all pesticides for safety and effectiveness, and operates strict follow-up controls over their supply and use.

R and D	Research and Development.
Regulatory Appraisal Guide	Produced by the Better Regulation Unit, Cabinet Office in 1997. This booklet offers general guidance to policy makers on Regulatory Appraisal.
Research Councils	Bodies established by Royal Charter, funded principally from the science budget, and charged with supporting research and postgraduate training.
Ring-fencing	Allocating money to local authorities on the basis that it can only be used for funding a specific function.
Risk Assessment	The scientific evaluation of known or potential adverse health effects resulting from human exposure to foodborne hazards.
Risk Communication	An interactive process of exchange of information and opinion on risk among risk assessors, risk managers and other interested parties.
Risk Management	The process of weighing policy to accept, minimise or reduce assessed risk and to select and implement appropriate options.
Scottish Food Co-ordinating Committee	A multi-disciplinary group with members from local government, central government and professional associations for the co-ordination of the enforcement of food law in Scotland and liaison with LACOTS on UK matters.
SEPA	Scottish Environmental Protection Agency.
Single Liaison Body	Under the Additional Food Control Measures Directive 93/99/EEC, each Member State has a nominated single liaison body, whose role is to improve inter-state co-operation and provide an efficient means of resolving transborder food complaints and investigations.
SPS (Sanitary and Phytosanitary)	Measures designed to protect animal plant and human health.
SVS	State Veterinary Service.
TBT	Technical Barriers to Trade.
Third countries	Any country or territory which is not part of the customs territory of the European Community.

VMD	Veterinary Medicines Directorate, an Executive Agency of MAFF. Responsible for the licensing and control of the manufacture and marketing of veterinary medicines, for the surveillance of residues in animal products, and for the monitoring of suspected adverse reactions to veterinary medicines in animals and humans.
VPC	Veterinary Products Committee.
WHO	World Health Organisation, a branch of the United Nations.
Zoonosis	An animal disease communicable to man.
Zootechnical feed additives	Antibiotics, growth promoters, coccidiostats and other medicinal substances when used as additives in feedingstuffs.

81

Printed in the UK for The Stationery Office Limited on behalf of the
Controller of Her Majesty's Stationery Office
Dd 5067760 1/98 48003 Job No 31939